MOUNTAIN OF
FEAR

Finding Peace after Sexual Abuse

Rachel Green

WESTBOW
PRESS*
A DIVISION OF THOMAS NELSON
& ZONDERVAN

Scripture quotations marked NIV are taken from the Holy Bible, New
International Version. NIV. Copyright 1973, 1978, 1984 by International
Bible Society. Used by permission of Zondervan. All rights reserved.

WestBow Press books may be ordered through booksellers or by contacting:

WestBow Press
A Division of Thomas Nelson & Zondervan
1663 Liberty Drive
Bloomington, IN 47403
www.westbowpress.com
1 (866) 928-1240

ISBN: 978-1-5127-8620-0 (sc)
ISBN: 978-1-5127-8619-4 (hc)
ISBN: 978-1-5127-8621-7 (e)

Library of Congress Control Number: 2017907458

Print information available on the last page.

WestBow Press rev. date: 05/15/2017

To my family and my angels here on earth
for their endless love and support

Preface

I have written this memoir for several reasons. The first reason is perhaps a little selfish in nature: I want my silenced voice to be heard. For so many years, I thought I had to be quiet and keep what happened to me a shameful secret. I thought that if I kept shoving it down and denying the effects on me, it would all go away and I'd be able to live a happy and normal life. After many years of trying to forget and move on, and failing to feel "normal," I finally realized I was never going to forget what happened and that the more I kept silent, the more ashamed I felt. I finally realized that in order to heal, I had to first fully acknowledge what happened and be honest about the emotional pain I felt. Then I had to regain control of my thoughts. When I keep silent, I let my abusers have control over my life and thoughts. It's like an infected toe: you can ignore the infection and the pain by covering it up with a sock and hope it heals. Or you can acknowledge that your toe is infected and painful and go to the doctor for treatment. Oftentimes, if you ignore an infected toe, it just festers and gets worse, eventually causing more damage throughout your body. The same goes for emotional pain. If it's not addressed, it will fester inside you, causing other issues in your life (addiction, self-hatred, relationship issues, and so forth). As a young child, I was unable to tell anyone the horrors I endured. Writing this memoir is my chance to give that child a voice and to live a life full of peace and free of shame.

I also want to document this incredible journey my family and I went on so that we will never forget the faithfulness of Christ and so we can pass the lessons we learned down to our children. This experience took my family and me on a journey up and down many mountain peaks. We saw the lowest valley of despair, experienced much needed mountain peaks giving us a glimmer of hope, came crashing down in frequent avalanches where we felt overwhelmed, and continued hiking when the dense fog rolled in, blinding our vision of what was ahead of us. But just like a real mountain hike, the dense fog quickly lifts and leaves a beautiful scene in front of you. This hike of ours was gut-wrenching, mind-blowing, and devastating to all of us, yet in the end, we have climbed to the highest summit and are so much stronger, full of peace, and appreciate all of God's blessings in our lives. In a world where many people give up hope when facing difficulties, it is my desire to give my children and nieces and nephews a ray of hope—to teach them what the apostle Paul said in Romans 5:3–5 (NIV): "Not only so, but we rejoice in our sufferings, because we know that suffering produces perseverance; perseverance, character; and character, hope. And hope does not disappoint us, because God has poured out his love into our hearts." It is my prayer that they will learn and believe wholeheartedly that with God's help, they can persevere through any trial, the deepest valley of despair, and be triumphant.

That same prayer goes for anyone who is suffering, whether from the pain of abuse, the heartache of watching a loved one suffering, or drowning in the darkness of depression. The journey my family and I experienced is such a powerful example of God's grace, which can be helpful not only for our own family but for so many other people as well. For the past several years, I have been sharing my experiences with my fellow colleagues during staff development days to discuss the effects of abuse on children. After every single presentation, I have always been asked, "How did you survive?" I can only answer, "By the grace of God!" The feedback I have received has always been so positive, and several people have come forward and shared their own histories of abuse. So my final reason for writing this book is to hopefully help others who have been abused, give them hope, and encourage them not to remain silent. I've been there, and I know the devastating effects that rape and abuse can have on someone … but I also know the peacefulness that comes from persevering through such an attack on one's psyche. I am more than a survivor. I am *thriving* in God's love and peace!

Here is my journey … You decide: was it a gift or a curse?

Acknowledgments

I want to acknowledge and thank my family for their support and help with the content of this memoir. This is a most complicated and confusing story, compounded by the fact that it happened two decades ago, and there are moments where I have very little recall of what happened. This memoir is written in the sequence of how things were remembered … The horrors I experienced as a little child were stuffed away and hidden in my unconscious mind until I was raped at the age of fifteen. The terror and emotional pain from being raped as a teenager brought forth the hidden memories of when I was only five years old.

When I was raped and my family was dealing with this trauma, my parents kept detailed notes, journal entries, and newspaper articles that greatly helped me piece this confusing puzzle together. I especially thank my mom for opening up her heart to me and allowing me to use her personal journal. In addition, I thank my parents and sister for letting me reopen those painful scars by letting me interview them about our darkest moments. When telling my story, I am also telling my family's story; rape affects the entire family, not just the victim. Throughout this memoir, I have included thoughts and journal entries from my family members to help paint a picture of what was all going on and how we all dealt with this trauma. My sister has been most supportive of my writing my story and has motivated me to follow through with my dream of writing a book about our experiences.

I apologize in advance for the graphic and violent content and for any triggers of your own painful memories. I did not include the details to shock you or garner pity. I included the violence and graphic details so that you will have a better understanding of the evilness I endured and why I reacted the way I did. When people hear the word *rape*, they may not realize or comprehend all the devastating effects it has on the victim or on the victim's family. They often just think of the physical act of rape; however, the emotional side effects of rape are much harder to heal from. It's my hope that when you read my memoir, you have a better understanding of rape and how it can imprison someone into silence and submission. Even though this experience happened more than two decades ago, I'm confident that with the detailed notes and journal entries, the information presented in this memoir is as accurate as possible. However, to protect my family, all names of people and places have been fictionalized.

Prologue

"No! I'm not going!" I yelled as I tightened my grip on the overstuffed beige chair. "I don't want to die. I don't want to kill myself ... I just don't know how to stop the pain!" I looked wildly around the room in search of anything I could use to throw at her to dissuade her from coming toward me.

"Rachel, it will be okay. It will be a safe place for you. I need you to be safe," Dr. McConnell said in a calm, quiet voice. Dr. McConnell reached out her hand in a reassuring gesture, attempting to calm my frenzied wild animal glances around the small therapist room.

I can't give in. I have to be strong. I have to be loyal, I kept telling myself silently. *Get away from me!* I was also screaming internally. As soon as Dr. McConnell moved an inch closer to me, the wild animal in me came out, thrashing at anything that threatened me. I felt as if I were being pushed up against the wall in the corner of a room that was slowly closing in on me. I felt I was being suffocated and trapped. I grabbed on to the armrest with a death grip and trembled as an earthquake of fear overtook my body.

"Rachel, I'm going to get your parents from the lobby and have you admitted to Harmony Mountains Psychiatric Hospital for your safety." As Dr. McConnell quietly left the room, I stared at the open door. As she and my parents returned to the room, Dr. McConnell explained, "You can either volunteer to go or you will be forced to go to the hospital. It's your choice. You can either get up and walk to your parents' car or you can wait for the paramedics to strap you to a gurney and take you there."

Buzzzzz. Click. The glass door slid open as my parents and I walked through the front doors of Harmony Mountains Psychiatric Hospital. We sat down in the front lobby. I didn't even know what to think. I sat in the plastic chair looking around the front lobby, absentmindedly picking at the bandage on my wrist. I didn't even remember slitting my wrist the night before. *How did I end up here? I was having the time of my life a few months ago, and now I'm sitting behind doors that buzz open and click when they lock me in. No one knows the pain I'm in. I have to keep pretending that everything is okay.* My sadness quickly dissolved into anger. *How could my parents take me to a place like this? How can they leave me here? Do they really think I'm crazy and need to be locked up like an animal? I hate them!*

"Rachel, time for you to say good-bye to your parents and to come with us."

Fine, I don't deserve to be part of the family anyway.

"So, Rachel, do you know why you're here?"

Well, yeah. My parents think I'm crazy and need to be locked up! "My parents and therapist think I'm suicidal," I responded with a quiet but respectful tone.

"Are you suicidal? Do you want to kill yourself?"

How dumb can these people be? Don't they ever listen? "No, I'm not suicidal. I've fought too hard to stay alive. I just don't know how to cope with what's going on. I'm dying inside, and I don't know how to end the pain."

If only I could explain how deep my pain is and how I curl up into a ball at night and cry on the inside. If only someone could see my quiet, invisible tears that I desperately want to let out but don't know how to. If only I could tell someone that I'm dying inside and need help. I'm dying inside, and nobody even knows it. But no, I can't talk about this. This is my problem, and I need to fix it on my own. I need to be loyal. I need to keep my family safe. I can never tell!

I tried to keep up the front that I was fine and that I didn't need help. I tried to act tough, but as the doctor asked me questions, I quietly slipped into a deep hole of desperation, despair, and hopelessness. I felt a heavy suffocating blanket was swallowing me.

As the blackness of despair washed over me, I heard the doctor gently say, "Well, let's start with looking at some pictures. I'll show you a picture and you tell me what you see."

As I looked at the first inkblot picture, I replied with a questioning voice, "All I see are some paint splatters."

"Yes, these are ink splatters, but what do the splatters look like to you?" The doctor kept pressing me for an answer. I cautiously looked again at the red and blue splotches. As the doctor flipped the next picture card onto the table for me to look at it, I began to panic.

No, no, no! I can't show my fear! I can't face it! I need to shove it back down. It's too scary! I can't breathe! Help me! "I see a girl and blood," I nervously answered, but I was suddenly paralyzed with fear as flashbacks sped before my eyes:

> *A gruesome crime scene photo is shoved in front of me, and as I look away, the photo is pushed up against my face. "What do you see?" he repeatedly yells at me. "Believe me when I say that this will be you if you ever tell anyone!"*

"Rachel, you need to tell me what you see," the doctor kept prodding me.

No! I won't ever tell! Ahhh! Just make these images disappear! Just stop! Every time the doctor asked what I saw in the inkblot pictures, the more terrified I became. I don't know if it was out of terror, out of stubbornness, or perhaps a little bit of both, but I was mute. I would not answer. I just stared at the doctor with a death stare ... a blank face ... a face void of emotion ... a lifeless stare.

Chapter 1

My childhood could be described as an episode on the *Leave It to Beaver* show. I grew up in what many people would describe as the perfect all-American family. My family was a happy and loving Christian family. I had two loving parents who were happily married, an older brother who was my best friend, a younger sister who looked up to me, a younger brother whom we all adored, and a faithful German shepherd mix dog. Both of my parents worked, but they were always around when we needed them. Dad was a pastor whose office was at home, and Mom was a stay-at-home mom who did day care in the home. Since Dad's office was in the basement of our house, he was always there, and Mom always had fresh homemade cookies or a cake waiting for us. My parents were very welcoming and had an open-door policy for our friends. If we had friends who needed a safe place to stay, they were welcome to stay with us.

Although we lived just a few miles from the inner city, we felt safe in our neighborhood. Yes, the street signs were littered with graffiti, a known drug house was just around the corner from our house, shoes were hanging from the highline wire to mark it as a drug neighborhood, and my parents called the police on a weekly basis, but we all felt safe. I was always thinking that since we didn't have bars on our windows, we lived in a safe neighborhood.

Abigail (my ten-year-old sister): Not knowing any different, I thought our neighborhood was great. I never felt unsafe in our neighborhood. We went on frequent walks and bike rides, with Mom pushing Ben in the stroller. I loved walking to the "junkyard park," a weird park with chain-link fences around trash turned into "sculptures." The only thing I was scared of was the road in front of church since it was so busy.

I was proud of our house. It was one of the largest houses on the block, the yard always looked trimmed and manicured (an elderly man from the church congregation would come and weed the sidewalk from our house to the church and the adjoining church parking lot with a butter knife on a weekly basis), and Mom always made the house and yard so pretty with all her flowers. Mom was super organized and enjoyed keeping the house clean, so I never had to worry what my friends would think or say when they came over to visit. In addition to my mom's bubbly personality and my dad's calm demeanor, the house and yard were pretty and welcoming. Our house was always a place of safety and love.

Growing up in a parsonage and being a pastor's kid had its perks and downfalls. One of the perks was that the elderly women in the church just adored us and "adopted" us as their grandchildren. Since we didn't have any relatives in the same state, the congregation quickly became our family. We became very close and attached to the congregation. One of my favorite memories is about going to Mr. and Mrs. Parson's house. They had a house built into the side of a steep hill and loved to garden. Whenever we went to their house, we ran up the stairs to the main level and made a beeline right to the aquarium, which was filled with cold clear water and thousands of smooth polished rocks. After plunging our hands into the cold water and sifting through the pile of beautiful stones, we each chose our special treasure to take home. We were then rewarded with a handful of candy and went outside to play while my parents visited with them. Their yard was like a yard I'd never seen before. It had a large garden with a fence around it, beautiful flower gardens everywhere you looked, flowerpots overflowing with a rainbow of colors, and rolling hills with the greenest, softest, spongiest grass I had ever seen. My siblings and I would take off our socks and shoes and run up and down the rolling hills while laughing and screaming. Sometimes we would feel sick from the continuous tumbling races down the hills, but I loved it when we visited the Parsons!

Another benefit of being the pastor's family was that we got to have our very own roller-skating rink. On Saturday mornings when my mom cleaned the church, my sister, little brother, and I turned the church basement into our own roller-skating rink. We would haul my large boom box, roller skates, and snacks across the backyard to the church. I would plug in my boom box and play my Amy Grant tapes at almost full volume, and if I felt daring, I would play my MC Hammer tape. It was great to have the entire basement to ourselves. My sister, Abigail, and I would skate as fast as possible, grab onto the metal support pole, whip around quickly, and skate to the next pole, trying to see how fast we could go past each other without crashing. Abigail would sing along with the songs with much gusto, while I just smiled and enjoyed the moment. Every once in a while, Mom would come downstairs to check on us and open her "concession stand." Mom would be in the church kitchen and we could "order" snacks at the counter by the serving window. I loved it when Mom was signed up to clean the church!

Despite being spoiled by the congregation, living in a parsonage was sometimes like living in a glass house. We had very little to no privacy and I felt that someone always knew what was going on. I felt I always had to be on my best behavior and be the perfect daughter. I felt as if all eyes were on us and that if we misbehaved, it would be a reflection on my parents' parenting. I remember Dad preaching, Mom singing in the choir, and my siblings and me sitting in the church pew by ourselves or with one of our adopted grandmas. When I got angry with my little sister or my older brother, I would sometimes sit with my arms crossed and sneakingly pinch her or him without moving my arms so that no one would notice that we were fighting. However, for the most part, I was a good girl and worked hard to live up to that perfect Christian daughter image. My parents never said we had to behave in a certain way or try to be the "perfect" Christian kids; I just put that pressure on myself. As my mom wrote in her journal:

Let me give you a brief character sketch of Rachel ... She was always on the quiet side but very caring. She always pushed herself to achieve good grades and to be good in sports. She had a lot of natural talent playing sports and loved that as her hobby. She was very responsible, and people loved to have her babysit for them. She loved playing with the children, and she would play fun games that she made up with them. She taught Sunday school at our church for the four-year-olds and helped with a young children's youth group. The parents and kids all loved Rachel. She was a wonderful example of a young Christian teen. She dressed very modestly and didn't pay much attention to music. Rachel wasn't interested in boys or talking on the phone. She was everything that a parent could want in a teenager.

Abigail: Rachel and I played a lot! She always had imaginative ideas ... Oftentimes, she would come up with an idea that would take all day to set up. We used to set up the whole basement as a store ... My favorite was when we played pet store. We'd keep the "horses" in the fenced-in area around the furnace. I loved that white fence around the furnace. In my mind, it was exactly like a horse corral! And we had that big book with all the different dog breeds; we'd circle which ones we wanted to buy. We'd use all our stuffed animals. Rachel was always so creative with setting things up, but I think with her being five years older, she'd get bored once we started playing. She'd leave me with all the cleanup. As Rachel got older, there was a gradual shift from playing make-believe with me to her getting more active at school. I began to play more with our little brother, Ben.

Chapter 2

Being a pastor's kid, I had attended parochial schools every year until the start of sixth grade. I was so excited (yet nervous) to start a new year at the nearby public school. In order to diversify the schools, the public school district offered families two choices when it came to enrolling their children. Parents could choose to have one child attend a school in the ghetto, and the other children in that family could attend a school in their neighborhood. Or families could choose to put their children's names in a lottery and have their children attend a school that was randomly picked. After much deliberation, my parents chose to have my older brother be the "sacrificial lamb" and attend the public school deep in the ghetto so that I could attend the nicer, safer school in our neighborhood.

My mom knew a teacher at the middle school I was going to attend, and she was able to get me enrolled in the Discovery Program (a program for gifted students). Usually, students needed to be tested before they were enrolled, but I was given special permission to start at the beginning of sixth grade. I absolutely *loved* my new school! The sixth graders were housed in portable classrooms located behind the school. There were three rows of four portable classrooms, making it look like a war camp, and the students often referred to it as the "refugee camp." Even though the portable classrooms were talked down upon, I thought it was fun and I liked having our own "cabin." I was in P15, which was a double classroom, so it was twice as big, had twice the students, and had two full time teachers. My teachers even brought their dogs to school every day and we took turns walking them, sweeping the front stoop of our "cabin," and keeping our classroom clean. I easily made friends, and my friend Diana and I became very close. As the year went on, I became more and more outgoing and enjoyed getting involved in school activities and community sports teams.

For seventh grade, I was placed in a different homeroom than my best friend, Diana. I was disappointed that Diana and I weren't in the same homeroom, but I was excited that I got the homeroom teacher that many students loved and adored. Instead of being a classroom teacher, he was the director of student affairs and was in charge of placing students in various classes. Since I was never tested to be part of the Discovery Program, it was his duty to assess me. During homeroom, he would take a few students, one at a time, into the library for interviews and assessments. At first, I thought it was cool that I got to leave homeroom.

Once we were in the library, he sat me down at the table and began interviewing me. I really wanted to be in the Discovery Program since all my friends were enrolled in it and we would have all our classes together for the next two years. I wanted to impress him with how smart and quick-witted I could be. He rattled off the questions in record time, and seeing that he was holding a stopwatch, I felt the pressure to answer the questions as quickly as possible; I didn't even have time to think before answering.

"Tell me all about you. What do you enjoy doing? Tell me about your family. Tell me about your other school. What is your greatest fear? What do you secretly want to do even though you know it would get you in trouble? What would you do in this situation ..."

How can I answer some of these questions? I don't remember. I don't remember my previous school or my friends at that school. What's wrong with me? Why can't I remember my previous school? Why can't I even remember fifth grade? Why can't I remember things from my childhood? Why can I only remember sixth grade? I must be dumb. I must have a memory problem. I'm so stupid. I probably won't make it into the Discovery Program. As he frowned and shuffled through the papers in my file, I could tell he was disappointed with some of my answers. To my amazement, he actually granted me permission to continue in the Discovery Program!

As the year progressed, I became quite attached to a shy, withdrawn girl named Stacy. She didn't have many friends and was often picked on. I felt sorry for her and quickly became her friend. I didn't realize how manipulative and possessive she could be. Without even realizing it, I slowly stopped hanging out with all my friends. I spent all my time with her. We ate lunch together at our own table in the corner of the cafeteria. When my other friends said hi to me, I would smile and start to get up to visit with them. However, Stacy would scowl at me and start crying that I couldn't leave her and that I was all she had. I didn't even realize she was pulling me into her self-pity, her isolation trap.

After school, we would walk to her house and watch Disney movies. She was obsessed with Disney, and even though I felt they were too juvenile, I watched them with her anyway. Several times her dad, Detective Clark, who was a respected homicide detective, would come home while we were watching movies. He explained that he was tired and stressed from his job as he poured himself a mixed drink of orange juice and vodka. After shrugging his shoulders, he got down two more glasses from the kitchen cabinet and began making two more mixed drinks. He handed them to us and said, "Enjoy. I won't tell if you don't tell!"

I really shouldn't drink it. This is wrong. What should I say? Maybe just one little sip ... Mmmmm. This is pretty cool! Being served an alcoholic drink and I'm only in seventh grade! I was surprised by how easily the drink went down and how much I enjoyed it.

I can't believe I just drank it. I know it's wrong. I'm so ashamed. My parents are going to be so disappointed. Watching Disney movies with Stacy and having mixed drinks with her dad quickly became the routine.

One day while Stacy and I were downstairs watching the movie *Hook*, Detective Clark came down the steps holding a manila folder in one hand and his mixed drink in the other hand. He went into the small closet under the stairs where they kept all their movies and then called me to join him. I had no idea what he wanted, so I got off the couch and went to the closet. In the closet, the back wall was lined with movies and there was a wooden TV tray set up with a brown wooden chair behind it. He told me to sit in the chair. It was back in the far corner, and while moving the TV tray out of the way, it bumped against the movies.

"Are you drunk, Rachel? Look at you—you can't even handle your alcohol!" he sneered at me.

I'm not drunk! Yes, I had one or two drinks, but I'm perfectly fine! This is just a tight area! Maybe I am drunk! What will my parents say? I'm so dumb. I shouldn't be drinking!

As I sat down in the cramped space facing him as he sat on the other side of the TV tray, I suddenly realized just how small this space was. I felt trapped in the corner and very nervous as I studied his balding head with just a small patch of graying brown hair on each side of his head. He took off his brown suit coat and draped it on the back of his chair, exposing his shoulder gun holster with the butt of his gun showing. He casually leaned back in his chair and gently tossed the manila folder onto the TV tray. He instructed me to open it as he nonchalantly folded his hands behind his head. I opened the file and saw gruesome crime scene photos.

I can't look at these! I think I'm going to throw up! I quickly closed the folder, bewildered why he would have me look at them.

"Rachel, open the file folder," Detective Clark quietly but firmly commanded. "What do you see?" I tried to avoid looking at the photos, but he shoved them in my face.

I answered, "I see a girl who looks like she was murdered."

"Keep looking, Rachel. Tell me all the details you see." I looked at him, thinking this was strange and that he was scary. I nervously described what I saw in the pictures. "That's right, Rachel. She is dead. Believe me when I tell you this: that will be you if you ever tell." He shoved the open file toward me and nonchalantly finished his drink, got up, grabbed his jacket, and left.

What in the world just happened? What was that all about? Is it the drinking I'm not supposed to talk about? That was creepy! I carefully got up from my chair and went back to watching *Hook* with Stacy. She was so involved in watching the movie that I don't even know if she knew I was gone for a few minutes!

As the year went on, my homeroom teacher would occasionally have me, Stacy, and a boy named Sebastian join him in the library to "enhance our learning." At first it was very innocent, like practicing impromptu speeches and getting to know us on a more personal level. Eventually, he began talking about the history of wars around the world and how the countries used torture techniques to punish or interrogate prisoners of war. He would bring in weird artifacts and go into extreme detail how evil the torture was. He would then tell us the "secret" of how to outsmart the torture. He taught us how to dissociate from the pain to keep our sanity. He would pretend to hit us and watch our reactions; he would often hypnotize us and constantly fired questions at us.

Eighth grade was a continuation of seventh grade. I was still in the Discovery Program, and the only friends I hung out with at school were Stacy and Sebastian. The only time I got away from Stacy was when I was playing softball, basketball, and soccer for the community league. Playing soccer was my all-time favorite hobby. Even though our team rarely won, I still enjoyed the sport and the girls on the team.

During the end of seventh grade and beginning of eighth grade, I started a paper route. I loved my paper route and the responsibility of delivering papers on time, collecting money, and organizing my supplies. Meeting new people and persuading them to buy the newspaper was exhilarating. It gave me a new outlook on life and boosted my self esteem. I took this job very seriously and was even nominated for newspaper delivery person of the year. Since my family had a tight budget and lived paycheck to paycheck, I was determined to earn money and pay for my own clothes and any extras that I wanted. At the beginning of eighth grade, I signed up to go to Mexico with my Spanish club. I knew that I would appreciate my trip more if I paid for the entire trip myself and that my parents didn't have the money to pay for my trip, so I scrimped and saved every penny from my paper route.

I was desperate to earn enough money to pay for my trip, so I jumped at the chance to deliver packages for Detective Clark. Stacy and I would ride the city bus downtown to the humane society to look for a dog for her to adopt. On our way to the humane society, we would get off and walk a few city blocks to find the address we were given.

As we searched for the right address and walked past numerous people playing their guitars or other makeshift musical instruments along the building walls, several homeless men asking for money would confront us. I tried to not notice the foul odor of rotten food coming from the garbage bins, the frequent yelling coming from the buildings we passed, empty beer bottles and garbage strewn throughout the alley, and the inquisitive and glaring eyes of the homeless people sitting against the brick wall or sleeping in the doorways. Even though it was daytime, it was scary. We were so easily startled that we would jump and grab on to each other at every noise or whenever we saw someone run past us in the alley. However, we were on a mission and wouldn't stop until we got to the right warehouse to deliver Detective Clark's package.

We'd timidly go to the side door of the warehouse and do the secret knock that he taught us. After what seemed like an eternity, the door would slowly open and a man would emerge from the dark building. The man would pay us, and then we continued on to the humane society. Sometimes the man would be an older heavyset man, probably in his fifties, with brownish hair. He would always tell us to be careful. Other times, a sleazy-looking younger man, probably in his late twenties, would come to the door. He had jet-black hair slicked back into a ponytail, a pox-scarred skinny face, and always wore shiny black sunglasses. He'd harass us and talk about "his girls." He creeped us out, and Stacy and I referred to him as "Sleazeball" or "Greaseball."

When we got back to Stacy's house, Detective Clark would give each of us a cut of the money. After weeks of searching for the perfect dog for Stacy, we finally found a beautiful white German shepherd husky mix with blue eyes for her. Once she adopted this dog, our deliveries stopped. Detective Clark would often joke, "Do you realize how much dirt I have on you? You do know that you're my drug ponies, right?" I never knew if he was serious or joking. I never looked inside the packages, but it wouldn't surprise me if that was true. He knew I would never tell, since I felt so ashamed for the frequent underage drinking and lying to my parents. Plus, he often "shared" detailed stories and photos from his homicide cases and would even have me role-play certain circumstances so he could better understand the case. Sure, he creeped me out and I was scared of him, but I could never tell my parents! Why would they believe me? I'd get in trouble for drinking.

I don't want to end up dead in one of his crime scene photos! His secret is safe with me.

Chapter 3

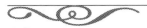

During seventh and eighth grade, Stacy, Sebastian, and I all took Spanish class together. Every student in Spanish class chose a Spanish name, and I chose the name Rosalita. During Spanish class, Stacy, Sebastian, and I sat at the same table. I was usually a serious student and wanted to please the teachers, but when I was around Sebastian, I often joked around and did more playing than listening and learning. Sebastian was a jolly, funny roly-poly boy. His parents were from Mexico and only spoke Spanish at home. His brother was involved in a gang, his home life wasn't great, and he avoided being at home at all costs. He was fun to be with, always made me laugh, and was in desperate need for friendship or belonging. I felt sorry for him since he had such a sad home life, and I enjoyed his company. Even though he was fluent in Spanish, he chose to take Spanish to fulfill his foreign language requirement. I would tell him that I needed to listen and pay attention during Spanish class, but he kept saying that I'd do fine and that he could help me with Spanish. When it came to taking a test or quiz, I'd panic since I realized that I missed most of the instruction due to goofing around with Sebastian and Stacy. Sebastian saw that I was panicking and would push his paper closer to me so that I could look at his answers and whisper the answers to me. If I wouldn't have cheated, I'm sure I never would have passed Spanish class.

Since our Spanish teacher would only call on us in our Spanish names, I often felt that when I was Rosalita, I was the fun, rebellious girl. Spanish class was the only time I felt I could let my hair down and have fun. The rest of the time, I was very serious and felt I had to be the perfect student and daughter. The more I drank and lied to my parents, the more pressure I put on myself to hide that part of me and be the perfect daughter. Even though I often felt torn up inside for cheating and playing during class, it was a welcome release of stress.

With Sebastian's help, I was able to pass Spanish and was allowed to go to Mexico with the Spanish club. The summer between eighth and ninth grade, nine other students and I went to Mexico for seventeen days. While in Mexico, I kept my Spanish class persona alive. I often thought of myself as Rosalita and was the daring, flirtatious girl. I definitely came out of my shell. I had been friends with Sebastian for the past two years, and we had grown to be good friends. I enjoyed being with him since he made everything fun and he always got me to laugh. We would have fun, but we often got in trouble. For example, one day while Stacy and I were working on a school project at the nearby public library, Sebastian came into the library and started shooting us with a water gun. At first, I tried to ignore him. That didn't work, so then I tried to get him to stop since a librarian kept looking at us with a stern face. By this time, Stacy and I were both laughing and trying to avoid getting wet. Eventually, Sebastian gave both of us water guns and we ended up having a water gun fight in the library. We ran and darted behind the bookshelves, shooting at each other between the stacked books on the shelves and hiding from the librarian who was yelling at us. Understandably, we got kicked out of the library.

During our trip to Mexico, Sebastian started flirting with me and wanted to take our friendship to the next level. I was flattered that he was flirting with me, and I enjoyed his attention. I didn't have any interest in having a boyfriend, but I can't deny that I enjoyed his attention and that I egged him on. I would flirt back but kept shutting him down when he asked if we could be boyfriend and girlfriend. I would laugh at him when he asked me to be his girlfriend, but I continued to flirt with him. At the time, I didn't realize how serious he was about liking me. I was enjoying just being friends and practicing flirting with him. Being quite naive about the whole dating thing, I didn't realize just how mean and hurtful I was being. I thought we were just having fun and that he knew I just wanted to be friends.

After a long day of sightseeing and touring Mexico City, most of us would go to our hotel rooms before curfew and pretend to be sleeping for the night. Once we knew that Senorita Gomez was sleeping, we would sneak out of our rooms and go to the hotel bar. Since there was no drinking age, we were served alcoholic drinks with no questions. We spent several hours drinking and dancing and then snuck back to our hotel rooms.

One night while sneaking back to my hotel room after drinking and dancing, Sebastian and I got stuck in an elevator. It was a stormy night, and the power went out, leaving just the two of us in a dark, stuffy elevator. At first, Sebastian and I thought it was funny. I screamed with laughter as he tried to scare me by rocking the elevator back and forth. The nervous excitement of being trapped in a dark elevator in a foreign country quickly dissolved. Being intoxicated, I was quite flirtatious, and Sebastian took advantage of the situation. He pressed himself against me and pushed me up against the wall. He began kissing me, and I laughed at him while pushing him away, saying I would never kiss him and that we were just friends. He was insulted and got mad. This was the first time I had ever seen him angry. His anger surprised me since in the past, he had always laughed and kept on flirting with me even after I told him no. I guess I had let him down one too many times. I tried to change the subject by calling for help: "Ayudame! Ayudame!" Sebastian joined me and we continued yelling for help.

As the minutes ticked by, we both were beginning to get scared. The elevator was getting stuffier. It seemed as if the blackness was getting darker and darker, and we couldn't ignore the gentle swaying of the elevator anymore. We heard a lot of thumps and men yelling in Spanish. After what seemed like an eternity, we finally heard men talking to us in Spanish through the elevator walls. Sebastian understood them and said they were going to find a crowbar to pry us out. A little while later, we saw the yellow glow of a flashlight beam as the elevator doors were being pried open. Through the dim light, we saw that although the doors were open, instead of looking out into the hallway, we were staring at a black cement wall. We were stuck between floors, so the Mexican hotel workers had to take hold of my outstretched arms and pull me up several feet and through an opening onto the next hotel floor. I was so relieved to be pulled out and being able to sit on the tile floor of the hotel hallway. As I watched Sebastian being pulled out, I saw Senorita Gomez running toward us with a flashlight. She was worried since she couldn't find us and no one else knew where we were. She was relieved to have found us, but once she found out that we had gone to the hotel bar, we were then sequestered to our hotel rooms and had an earlier curfew for the rest of the trip.

Our last night in Mexico City, Sebastian, several other students, and I were in Sebastian's hotel room playing cards. We were having fun at first, but then Sebastian got sad that we wouldn't be all together since we were going to be staying in a different town with various host families. In the middle of a card game, he started throwing the cards out the tiny open slats of the window. I went over to the window and watched the cards float to the ground and get run over by the passing cars. I was so angry with him. I wanted to keep playing cards, and I didn't like it that he ended the game. He became all depressed and said that it didn't matter since he was like the cards and that I was just tossing him aside. He was upset that I wasn't giving him attention. I just kept thinking, *What's with Sebastian all of a sudden? What's his problem?* I decided that it was time to leave, and I went back to my hotel room.

A few minutes later, there was a knock on my door. I was told that Sebastian was suicidal and that he was threatening to jump off the patio if I didn't come back and see him. I ran back to his hotel room and saw him standing on the other side of the patio railing, holding onto the railing and crying. Mind you, we were on the seventeenth floor of a hotel in the middle of Mexico City, a very busy city. As the cars were rushing by and I heard horns beeping, I kept thinking it would be my fault if he let go and fell into the street and got run over. I kept thinking of the playing cards floating to the street below and being run over. I couldn't let Sebastian get hurt. I rushed out to the patio and told him, "I'm so sorry! I'm so sorry! Please come back over here!"

He tearfully responded, "Do you love me? Will you be my girlfriend?"

I hastily screamed, "Yes! Just climb back over here! Hurry!" Sebastian climbed back over the railing, hugged me, and gave me a kiss on my cheek. I was so mad at him and yelled, "What kind of stupid stunt was that? What were you thinking?"

"I just love you so much. I can't stand knowing that we won't see each other as much the next week. I wanted to see if you care about me," he tried to explain. I just left the hotel room, mad that he would involve me in such a scary situation, mad at myself for causing him to do such a stupid thing, relieved that he wasn't hurt, and ashamed for leading him on to this point.

The trip to Mexico was a trip I'll never forget. It was more than just a learning experience; it was the beginning of my new life. It opened my eyes to living life. I came home with a new spirit … I was much more outgoing, and I was determined to make friends and escape Stacy's trap. I embraced the joy and happiness from my newfound freedom. I loved the freedom and independence I had in Mexico. I felt so grown up and capable of doing everything by myself. I came home a changed person.

Mom: The trip to Mexico seemed organized, but as parents, the one thing we felt uncomfortable with was the very strict policy that students could not call home and could not talk to their parents for the seventeen-day trip. Senorita Gomez said an occasional phone call would prompt homesickness. She stressed that when your children came home, they would be like a changed person. She said not to expect them to talk to you right away, saying that the trip really changes them. That troubled me, but I felt a trip like this would probably teach Rachel to be independent and more mature. While they were in Mexico, they stayed with host families. Each student filled out a questionnaire with a lot of information that was given to the host families. We received no information and didn't even know the names of the host families. We were told these host families had been doing this for years and they were all approved through the college that sponsored the program. When Rachel came home from Mexico, she was extremely talkative, and from what the other kids said, it sounded as if she was the life of the party. I was embarrassed because that was not the Rachel I knew at all.

Chapter 4

Fall 1993

"Watch out!" Jenna screamed as we jumped over the muddy ditch, just nearly missing being run over by a dark blue sports car. "What just happened?" we asked each other as the car went squealing past us. We continued walking back to school after playing a soccer game against a nearby private school.

I'm sure the sight of us both covered in mud, with our braided hair twisted into knots and carrying our large duffel bags, was quite humorous. We nervously kept walking, looking over our shoulders and watching for any more crazy drivers to run us off the road again. Busy talking and laughing, we didn't notice at first that the same dark blue sports car was quietly following us. As we turned the corner, we saw that the car had returned and was following us. We began to run, our braids tied into knots coming undone, making our braids flap on our backs, our duffel bags weighing us down and bumping into the back of our legs as we tried to run through the slippery mud and jump out of the way.

The driver, who was about our age, revved the engine. We had no place to go as the car came zooming at us and then screeched to a stop right in front of us. A dark-haired, pale-skinned boy wearing a white hooded sweatshirt rolled down the passenger side window. He yelled out the window, "Hey, aren't you Rachel?"

I had never seen this boy before, and besides being scared of almost being hit by a crazy driver, I was bewildered how he knew my name. I had no idea what school he went to or who he even was—how did he know who I was?

I nervously answered, "Yes, that's my name."

He immediately replied, "I've been studying you," and then he sped off.

Jenna and I looked at each other in disbelief. *Who is this guy? What did he mean that he's been studying me?* We tried to laugh it off and talked about the game. By the time we got back to our school, we decided not to tell our parents in fear that they wouldn't let us walk by ourselves. Quite honestly, I didn't give this incident much thought after that day.

Playing soccer was the joy of my life. I loved being on the varsity soccer team and playing with all the upperclassmen, being able to make a name for myself. I felt as if I belonged. Even the senior girls respected my playing ability, and I was proud of the fact that I was the highest scorer on the team—and I was just a freshman! The girls on the team were a close bunch, and we often braided our hair and then twisted the braids into knots, calling ourselves the "Twisted Sistas." We had fun together and looked out for each other. We had a fun coach who kept the atmosphere lighthearted and fun.

Kicking the ball as hard as I could and watching it go into the net was exhilarating. It was my personal goal to score a goal every game. I was determined to accomplish my goal. I wouldn't let anything get in the way. I didn't care if we were behind by several goals and only had a little time left. I never gave up. My determination scared my teammates and my opponents. I had that look in my eyes that told everyone I was determined to score and that I wouldn't back down. I didn't care that I had played the entire game and was dead tired; I had to score. I ended the season almost achieving my goal.

There were only two games where I didn't score. At the awards ceremony, Coach Andrews said that even he was scared to go up against me during practice, adding that I played with such determination even in practice. I never could explain my need to score every game. I just felt that I had to. Soccer was my high—the great feeling of being included on a team, the natural high I got from running and kicking the ball and watching it go into the net, and kids at school talking about me and giving me high fives in the hallways. I thought life was great. I couldn't have loved high school more. I was getting all As in my honor classes, I was making lots of new friends, I was successful in soccer, and boys were noticing me. Life couldn't get any better!

I was involved in various school activities such as being on the freshman homecoming decorating committee and going around collecting money for the penny wars. I was outgoing and enjoyed being in the company of various people. I loved being friends with people in various groups. I was friends with the studious students, the people involved in music groups, athletes, and people from different ethnic groups. I felt I had no boundaries … I could be friends with whomever I wanted, and I loved learning things from each different group. It was so freeing to be away from Stacy! I was still her friend, but I didn't hang out solely with her. Rather, I spent most of my time with my friends Jenna and Ana. They both lived in my neighborhood and came from tough home situations. When they needed a safe place to stay, my parents graciously welcomed them to stay with my family. Yes, we spent most of our time together, but they weren't possessive like Stacy. Although the three of us were often together, we also had other friends we were comfortable hanging out with. Jenna, Ana, and I looked out for each other and would do anything to help each other out.

Even though I was still serious about my grades, I was silly, known for having fun, and was flirtatious. I thrived on the attention I was getting from my friends, boys, and my brother's friends. My brother Luke was two years older than I was, and we would often play sports together with his friends and stay up late at night playing Ping-Pong. I loved how they included me. I loved hanging out with juniors while I was just a freshman. I loved high school and thought nothing could ever go wrong. I was invincible. Life as I knew it was great!

Homecoming at my high school wasn't a big deal. People would just wear jeans and a nice shirt; only a few girls wore dresses. Part of the festivities was a talent show. My brother and his friends dressed up as Vanilla Ice and performed for the school. Luke has always loved the spotlight, and their performance was outstanding! I was so proud of my brother and his friends.

I had many guy friends, but I wasn't dating any certain guy. I was still friends with Sebastian and had decided to go to the homecoming dance with him and his older brother, Juan, and his girlfriend, Alyssa, who was Stacy's sister. Sebastian picked me up at home, and my mom welcomed him in. As soon as he walked into our house, the entire house reeked of the cologne samples my mom had given him previously. Instead of just dabbing it on, it smelled as if he had soaked his clothes in it. As we walked to his brother's silver-and-maroon striped Astro minivan, Sebastian tried to hold my hand. I wasn't ready to be anyone's girlfriend and felt too self-conscience to let him hold my hand, so I just kept walking and shrugged out of his hand grasp. It had always grossed me out to watch girls at school with their boyfriends. I hated watching the girls act as if they were just an item to be owned. I had seen too many girls give up their own identities and do whatever their boyfriends wanted to do. I was determined not to date and act like that!

The ride to school was fun as we all talked about the different talent show acts. Once we got to school and Juan parked the van, I asked Sebastian, "Are you ready to have fun tonight?"

He replied by smiling and putting his right arm over my shoulders and pulling me toward him. With his left hand, he reached into his jeans pocket and pulled out a condom packet. I couldn't believe what I was seeing and pulled away from him. "I'm always prepared for a fun night!" he replied with a smirk.

Oh, no! Ahhh! What do I say? Absolutely not!

"You're not going to need that tonight!" I replied with a laugh, jumping out of the van.

We walked through the metal detector and entered the cafeteria, where the dance was taking place. Students were laughing and having a good time, rap music was blaring, strobe lights were flashing, and I was mesmerized by all of it. I couldn't believe I was at a high school dance. It was so exciting!

Sebastian and I found some of our friends and danced several fast songs. A guy bumped into me and motioned for me to follow him. As

I followed him out to the dark courtyard, Ana tagged along behind us. He held out his hand, and I saw that he had several little strips of paper with pink and gray on the ends. He put one on his tongue and gave me one. He said it would dissolve on my tongue and that I would have the best night ever. I thought it was candy, and I was about to put it on my tongue when Ana grabbed my arm and yelled, "What are you doing, Rachel? He just gave you angel dust!"

I couldn't believe how dumb I was. Instead of taking it, I tossed it into the garbage can. The guy shrugged his shoulders and left to find his next naive victim.

"See that guy over there?" Ana asked. "He's having a bad trip. He took some of that angel dust and now look at him! That stuff is scary … You never know if you'll have a good or a bad trip," Ana explained.

The poor kid was sitting outside all alone in the dark courtyard. He was sitting on the cement, back against the wall, with his head between his legs. He was crying, and his breathing was out of control. He kept grabbing and pulling his hair and picking imaginary things off his face. The sight of this poor kid experiencing his trip would scare anyone straight. I was so thankful for Ana! It was pretty humbling to know how naive I was. Seeing how lonely and scared that kid was made me realize how important it is to have good friends. I thought I knew how to take care of myself … I thought I knew the dangers … I thought wrong.

We went back inside and danced some more. A slow song played, and Sebastian asked me to dance with him. We started dancing, and then he placed his hand on my butt as we were dancing. I backed away in surprise. Juan was instantly next to us and explained that he had bet Sebastian I wouldn't allow him to touch my butt. I was angry that they were placing bets on me. Sebastian apologized, and we began dancing again. I teasingly asked him, "So what was the bet worth?"

"Five bucks," he replied.

Hmm … it's just touching my butt. No big deal. I shrugged and placed his hands on my butt, smiling at Juan. Juan gave Sebastian the five dollars when the song ended.

Before I knew it, the dance was over and Sebastian was walking me to his brother's van in the school parking lot. When we got to the van, he took my shoulders and pinned me against the side of the van. *Why is he acting this way? He's scaring me. Is that alcohol I smell on him?*

"We could continue the fun tonight. Just you and me," he whispered in my ear as he kissed my neck.

I'm so dumb. Why do I keep flirting with him? I don't like him that way! He's just my friend! I would never have sex with him! I'm so stupid! How do I let him down easily so he doesn't go psycho on me?

I nervously giggled, "It's time to take me home. Maybe some other time." *Oh no! Why did I just say that? Why did I give him hope for some other time? I am so stupid!*

Sebastian pouted and pretended to be heartbroken. I slid open the van door and quickly jumped in. Sebastian was quiet and sulked the whole way back to my house, where Juan dropped me off.

Chapter 5

Basketball season 1993

Toward the end of the soccer season, the girls' varsity basketball coach, Coach Carl, began to watch soccer practice. At the end of practice, he would call me over to talk. He said he was impressed with my playing ability and that he liked my determination. He asked if I thought about trying out for basketball. I told him I didn't know yet and that I didn't really enjoy basketball. He kept talking about the basketball program and how great it was, saying I would enjoy the sport and being on the team. He even went as far as to tell me that if I went to tryouts, he would put me on the varsity team. I just laughed and said that he didn't know what he was talking about since he hadn't even seen me play. He said he didn't need to see me play since I had the determination he was looking for. After every practice that he came to watch, he would pester me and ask if I decided to try out for basketball. I could tell he was getting frustrated since I always told him I didn't know yet.

While in the locker room getting changed after a soccer practice, I asked several of the older girls if they were going to try out for basketball. Some of the older girls laughed and said, "That would be the last thing I'd do! He's mean!" Other girls said that they were going to try out. I didn't know Coach Carl, so I didn't know who to believe. Some of the girls seemed to hate and fear him, while the other girls enjoyed being on the basketball team. I liked to make my own judgments, and I was thrilled about the possibility of maybe being on another varsity team as a freshman, so I decided to try out for basketball. I was starting to fantasize about being the top scorer and seeing all the newspaper articles about my playing ability. It was a great fantasy, and with Coach Carl's promise, it seemed it was highly possible.

As soon as I started to attend basketball tryouts, I knew that Coach Carl had very different coaching techniques than my soccer coach. Again, being quite naive, I thought that maybe this was how varsity high school teams were taught. Coach Andrews was laid back and cared more about his players loving the game of soccer, and sometimes he was even ridiculed about how easygoing he was on his players.

Coach Carl, on the other hand, did more yelling and humiliating his players than actually teaching us how to play basketball. I don't remember him saying anything positive or encouraging to us the entire season. He was always yelling at us to do better, to put more effort into everything we do, saying that we were lazy and needed to work much harder. Since he was so demanding, I secretly hoped that I wouldn't make varsity. Rather, I enjoyed how the JV coach, Alex, worked with us, and I hoped that I could play for him. When the team roster was hung up on the locker room door, I was disappointed when I saw my name on the varsity team list. All the other girls who made varsity were happy and giving each other high fives. I wanted to be a part of the team, so I put on a smile and tried to be excited.

Basketball was fine at first. At times, I even enjoyed being pushed harder and expected to play well. I think the whole team rose to the challenge and improved since Coach Carl expected and demanded near perfection from us. But as we got closer to the first game, he began to go overboard with his expectations. If we missed a shot or had the wrong shooting positioning, he would hit us behind our knees with a rod, making the player fall to her knees. While running "suicide ladders," he would throw basketballs at us, telling us we always needed to be ready. If we ducked, flinched, or got hit by a ball, he would run over to the girl, yelling and swearing at her and pushing her down to the gym floor. He would scream that she was stupid, worthless, lazy, no good, and a disappointment to the team. If he ever caught us watching him belittle a teammate, the people watching would also be punished.

In addition to his harsh coaching techniques, I thought it was odd that he would keep accurate records of each girl's menstrual cycle. Coach Carl told us that he wanted to keep us safe and to prevent unnecessary injuries, explained that when we're on our periods, we are more apt to sprains and torn muscles. Even though I was uncomfortable sharing this information with him and thought it was odd, I did as he asked. Since none of the other girls questioned him, I began to believe that he was being extra careful and attentive to our health. I believed that he cared about us and that he had every right to know this personal information.

During one practice before the first game, I was pulled aside to talk to Coach Carl and Alex. They explained that I would be on both the JV and the varsity team so I could get more playing time. I asked how this would work, being on both teams. They said I would sometimes practice with the JV team, but that I would mostly practice with the varsity team. I would play two or three quarters of the JV game and then two or three quarters of the varsity game. They said my obligations would be primarily for the varsity team. I was thrilled! I was so happy to be able to play on the JV team with my friends and a nice coach like Alex. I was the only freshman on varsity, and the other girls didn't include me in their conversations or activities. I felt withdrawn and isolated from the team. All my fantasies of being the top player had vanished. Now I was just hoping I wouldn't be the laughingstock of the team!

When I played for varsity, I was nervous and unsure about my playing ability. I made careless mistakes and was so nervous I couldn't enjoy the game. When I played for JV, it was a complete change. I was included on the team, felt needed, enjoyed the company of the other girls, and *loved* playing for Alex. I felt confident in my playing ability, played well, played hard, and I enjoyed the game. I felt free when playing for JV. I was hoping that Coach Carl would say that I wasn't good enough for varsity and just let me play JV. Such was not the case.

A few days before the first basketball game, I saw "him" at practice. It was the same boy who almost ran Jenna and me over when we were walking home from the soccer game! He was talking to Coach Carl, and I was surprised to see him here since I had never seen him at school before. I was curious who he was and what he was doing at practice. They seemed like good buddies, for they were talking and laughing. The team soon found out that his name was Shawn and that he was going to be the trainer and scorekeeper/videographer.

From the day Shawn started helping out during practice, I could not get away from him. Now that I knew Shawn was a student at the same high school I went to, I started noticing him walking in the hall between classes. He was like my shadow, always one step behind me, following me wherever I went. It started to creep me out having him stalk me like that. I guess he really was studying me.

He was constantly hanging out by me, putting his arms around me and asking how his "chicka-babe" was doing. I hated being called that! He kept telling the other girls on the team that he had a secret crush on me and that we were almost married. He wasn't making any sense, and it bothered me that he was so possessive of me. *How could he say such things? I hardly even know him!* I kept telling him to leave me alone, but he only got more insistent.

Before long, Shawn began to harass me in the hallway between classes. He would get so angry when he saw me talking to my friend Travis or to any other guy. He demanded that I tell him everything I said to my guy friends and to promise him that I would only talk to him since I was his chicka-babe. I hated how he acted as if he owned me! The more possessive he became, the more I went out of my way to irritate him. I started to flirt more with my guy friends and hang out more with Travis. I wanted to prove to him that I had no interest in him and that I could do anything I wanted to do—he didn't own me!

It eventually got to the point where he was brave enough to approach me while I was with my friends. He would come up behind me, put his arms around my neck in what appeared to be a teasing headlock, and try to kiss me. I'm sure it appeared to be all in good fun, but it was no fun for me. I felt threatened when he would put me in a headlock like that and try to kiss me. I did not want to be kissed by him! My friends were confused because they had no idea who he was and why this "stranger" would act this way. I would constantly tell him no and to leave me alone, turning my head so he couldn't kiss me. He would not take no for an answer. He just got more insistent and forceful when he came up to me.

Our first game was against Shilah High School. I had played the JV game, and everything was fine. I enjoyed the excitement of playing and was excited to play my first varsity basketball game. Even though I didn't care that much about the game of basketball, the atmosphere is so exciting! All the fans are there cheering you on, the band is playing, the cops come and set up their watch on both ends of the gym to put out rival gang fights, and your feet and body feel the vibrations from the deep bass from the blaring music of the pre-game warm-ups. You can feel the adrenaline in the air!

After playing the JV game, I was sitting in the bleachers watching the boys' JV game with Stacy. And of course my shadow, Shawn, climbed up the bleachers and sat down right next to me. When Stacy went to buy a snack, I was left alone with Shawn. I was sitting there watching the game and trying so hard to ignore him that I didn't even realize he had his hand on my knee. When I glanced down and saw that his hand was indeed on my knee and inching farther up my thigh, pushing my shorts up, I jumped up in surprise and disgust and started to walk away. Before I could go far, he pulled me back down by him and told me nicely that he was just trying to stop me from shaking. I guessed the adrenaline from playing the game was still making me shaky. I couldn't believe that he was actually talking nicely to me and that he was supposedly trying to help me. *Maybe I overreacted and maybe he was just trying to help me stop shaking. I'm probably just overreacting!* I went back to watching the game. Pretty soon he had his hand on my thigh again. This time I knew I wasn't shaking. I told him to get his hands off me and to leave me alone. I told him there was no reason he had to have his hands on my leg. While I was arguing with him, Stacy came back with her popcorn. I was too upset to sit there and watch the game, so I went down to the locker room early to get dressed for the varsity game.

The next day was fine until lunch. Shawn continued to harass me and do his usual things, but then he added, "Wanna continue the fun?" I didn't know what he was talking about, so I asked him what fun he was talking about. "The fun we had at the basketball game last night," he responded. I didn't even know what to think or say back to him. I just turned around and went to 7-Eleven with my friends for lunch.

The first couple of games came and went with Shawn either at the scorekeeping table or at the top bleacher videotaping the game. During practices, he would join Coach Carl in humiliating the players and join in on the beatings. Sometimes they would say that a player needed a "special session" when she would do something wrong, no matter how miniscule the wrongdoing supposedly was. The "special sessions" would take place in the trainers' room with the door closed. I don't know what happened to the other girls, but I do know what happened to me during my sessions.

Once inside the room, Coach Carl would close the door, lock the door, put the key in his pants pocket, sideswipe my ankles, and push me down to the cement floor. He would yell and swear at me, telling me how worthless I was and how I needed to be taught a lesson. He would hold me down against the floor as he raised his fist and pretended to punch me. If I flinched or made the smallest movement, he would slap me across the face or punch me in the arm or stomach. He always told me to look him in the eye. I would look into his dark, almost black, eyes and see hatred and evil. As soon as I looked him in the eye, he'd strike me across the face. If I didn't look him in the eye, I would get backhanded. Whatever I did, I couldn't do anything to please him.

After being made to feel completely helpless, worthless, confused, and scared, he would force a Dixie cup of orange juice and his "special mix" down my throat and tell me to be a good girl and to be loyal to the team. He'd unlock the door, and I would hustle back to practice. It was an unspoken rule among the girls not to discuss those "special sessions." We were all a team, almost all of us being mistreated, yet we were all isolated. No one knew what happened behind the closed door, but we all knew what happened to ourselves and felt isolated in our own misery, not being able to talk about it with each other. Even though I knew my parents would be supportive of me, I felt as if I had to take care of myself. I was trying so hard to be self-reliant. I didn't want their help. I wanted to take care of myself, all by myself. *Besides, no one else is complaining. I must be over sensitive to his coaching methods.*

On game days, we would wear our warm-up pants and jackets to school to promote the game. It was always exciting on game days, and I felt special wearing the uniform during school. I loved being able to show off that I was on the varsity team. I hate to admit it that on game days, I would desert my friends in order to hang out with the girls on the team.

Despite the excitement and feeling proud of my uniform, I was hypervigilant since Shawn would come up behind me while I was walking to my next class. He would run up to me and try pulling my shorts and pants down. I was so embarrassed when one time he caught me off guard and pulled my pants and shorts halfway down, exposing my underwear. Thankfully, I was able to pull them back up before too many people noticed. The few students who saw what happened laughed at me, making me wish I could melt into the ground. The more I resisted his come-ons, the more annoying he became. The bullying increased. Shawn began tripping me and pushing me down the stairs, slapping me in front of other students, putting me in headlocks and choking me, and throwing me against the lockers. He was getting more and more violent. And I was just as stubborn to handle this on my own.

It was so frustrating since I knew other students and even teachers saw what was happening and how I was being mistreated, yet no one stepped in to help me or even tell Shawn to stop. I felt that since no one tried to help me, I was all alone in my misery and that I had no choice. I felt I had to rely on myself for protection. I had no trust in the teachers since they would walk right by me as I was cowering and covering my face to protect it from being hit, pleading with Shawn to stop. Sometimes the teachers would even glance at me and just continue walking into their classrooms.

I realize that our school had some serious gang issues and that there were constant gang fights involving weapons and people being pushed through the glass windows of the courtyard, and I know that the teachers themselves were probably scared of some of the students, but I still couldn't believe that they didn't help me! My parents and I later learned that my friend was dry raped by Shawn in front of her history teacher's classroom (the teacher finally reported this act several months later). Her teacher stepped right over her, went into her classroom, and shut the door, not even telling Shawn to get off my friend. How could the teacher ignore my friend crying for help and yelling at Shawn to get off her? Why were the teachers so scared to help us? I'm sure that Shawn felt he could get away with murder at the school.

Chapter 6

December 10, 1993

It was Friday night, and we were playing against a team that was farther away from home than any other team. Both the girls' JV and the girls' varsity teams were to ride together to the other school. As we were boarding the bus, I was so excited. This wasn't any ordinary school bus; we got to ride in a greyhound bus! There were comfy large seats, and we even had a bathroom on the bus. We were all so excited about this ride.

We played well and were excitedly talking afterward about the games we had just won. Most of the girls rode home with their parents or friends, so there were only a few of us who rode the bus back to school. On the way home, everything was fun for the first ten or fifteen minutes. We each had our own row of seats, and I was having fun talking with Kristin and Stacy. The three of us were in the rows way back by the bathroom, talking quietly and laughing. I was cold, so I stood up to put my warm-up pants on over my shorts. As I was doing this, Shawn walked to the back of the bus and acted as if he were going to go into the bathroom. We ignored him and continued talking. As I was reaching up to put my duffel bag back on the shelf above my seat, Shawn quickly slid into the seat next to me. Feeling irritated and frustrated that he was here, I told him to leave and to go back to his seat at the front of the bus. We were having fun talking girl talk, and I was so tired of him following me!

He kept saying that he was going to sit by me even if I didn't like it.

He pulled me down into the seat next to him and squeezed my wrists so tightly that I couldn't get away. He pulled me across his lap so that I was in the seat against the window. He pushed my head against the dark window and whispered in my ear that I better not even try to get away. As he pushed my head against the dark bus window, he grabbed my neck and sneered that he knew where all the pressure points were and that he could easily press on my neck and make me become temporarily paralyzed. He had used pressure points on me before, so I believed his threat and stopped fighting him. Since my face was pressed up against the window, I just stared outside at the dark night and watched the cars speed by us on the freeway. Everybody was in such a hurry; no one glanced up at the bus window to see how frightened I was. *Would anyone even notice if I was hurt? What is wrong with him? How can I get away from him? What's wrong with me? What did I do to him?*

He finally released his hold on my head. I tried so hard to ignore him and just keep talking to my friends. I didn't want him to know how scared I was of him. Kristin and Stacy kept talking with me, but I couldn't concentrate on what they were saying since Shawn was all over me, trying to kiss me and touch me. I kept thinking that I was glad that it was so dark in the bus and that they couldn't see what he was doing. I was so embarrassed. *Why is he doing this? Stop touching me! This is so embarrassing!* I didn't want to make a scene, so I didn't yell at him to stop, but instead I tried to elbow him and move away quietly. Stacy was sitting across the aisle from us, so I know she could see what was going on. Kristin was sitting in the row in front of Shawn and me, so she couldn't see us, but she could hear that we were struggling.

I realized that he was too strong for me to quietly get him to stop harassing me, so I tried a different tactic. When I get nervous, I have a nervous giggle. I'm sure this giggle sounded as if I were teasing and having a good time. However, I was scared and mad that I couldn't get him to stop touching me and kissing me. I kept telling him to stop and to leave me alone. I kept telling him to leave, saying that it wasn't funny. As he was kissing me and touching me, he whispered what he wanted to do with me. This is when I really began to panic. *What in the world? Seriously? Would he* really *try that on the bus with other people around? He must be crazy!* He began to pull on my pants to get them off. Luckily, when I saw Shawn coming back by us when I was putting my duffel bag away, I had tied my pants super tight. From experience, I knew that he liked to pull down my pants, so I always made sure they were tied extra tight when I was around him.

He was getting mad since he couldn't pull my pants off. I got a little louder and told him to stop. I saw Stacy looking at us as I struggled with Shawn. *I can't believe that you're just sitting there! I know you can see us! Why aren't you helping me? What kind of friend are you?* When Stacy saw me looking at her, she quickly looked away and put her head against her window and pretended to be sleeping. *So that's how you're going to be? Help me! I know you're just pretending to be sleeping! I can't believe you! What kind of friend are you?* Eventually, Kristin turned around and popped her head over the seat in front of us. She looked concerned and asked what was going on. Shawn took out his switchblade and pressed it into my side when she turned around. I so desperately wanted to yell for help, but feeling his knife, I knew I couldn't. I told Kristin that I was just trying to tell Shawn to leave me alone and that I wanted to sit somewhere else. Shawn pressed the knife harder into my side, so I stopped struggling with him. Shawn told her that we were just kissing and that he wanted some alone time with me. He told her to mind her own business since we were lovers wanting to be alone in the dark. She glanced at me and then slid back into her seat and put headphones on; she listened to music the rest of the way home.

Seriously? Stacy's pretending to be sleeping and Kristin is listening to music. Fantastic. How am I ever going to get away from Shawn? How can I get him off me? I can't believe my friends have left me all alone with this creep! The few other players on the bus were at the way front, talking and having a good time. I was so tempted to yell and make a run for it to the front of the bus, but I was too ashamed to yell out. *What did I do to make Shawn act like this?* I kept trying to get Alex's attention, but he and Coach Carl were talking in the very front row. I felt trapped—that I had no choice or way to escape.

Now that Shawn knew we would be left alone, he got even more persistent. He kept tugging on my pants and hissing at me to untie them. They were tied in a knot, so I couldn't undo the ties. Shawn got mad and took his knife and began to cut the inside hem of my pants in the crotch. He told me that if I didn't do what he wanted, then he would have to cut my pants and force himself on me. I had had enough. I was terrified when I saw that he had cut a large hole in my inner thigh of my warm-up pants. I thought he was really going to rape me there on that bus. I had to do something. *I can't believe this is happening to me! What is his problem? What did I do to him? I never even flirted with him—why is he acting this way? Help me! I'm too embarrassed to yell for help and make a scene, but someone please help! What can I do? What should I do?* As he was trying to undo his belt, I elbowed him in the chest and then kneed him in the nose as he bent over in pain. I quickly scrambled over him and slid into another seat. I looked back at him and saw him holding his nose and glaring at me. I don't know what scared me more, the evil hate-filled glare he gave me or knowing that paybacks are worse.

Even though I knew I would get punished for getting away and for hurting him, I was relieved that I was away from him. I kept my eyes forward the rest of the trip home, but I was on guard the whole ride, listening for him and being ready to run or fight if he came near me again. I was so tense that my body became sore. Thankfully, he left me alone the rest of the ride.

Chapter 7

December 13, 1993

The night of December 13 would be a turning point in my life and one of the most horrific nights in my whole life. After school, I went to basketball practice. I first checked in with the JV team, and Alex said they would end soon since there was a game the next day. He said there wouldn't be anything new to go over, so I went upstairs to the varsity gym for practice. I would have preferred to stay with the JV team, but I knew I would pay the consequences later if I didn't go to varsity. When I got upstairs, the other girls were in small groups, working on passing and shooting. I was afraid that Coach Carl would yell at me for being late, but he was busy looking at his notebook. I quietly joined the nearest group. I couldn't believe that Coach Carl didn't notice that I was late! I actually allowed myself to relax a little and just think about basketball.

He blew his whistle, and we all ran over to him. We reviewed one of the plays and practiced running it. Since he never yelled at us, he must have been satisfied, and he quickly dismissed us from practice. I felt this was one of my luckiest days—no one got yelled at, no one was beat, and we got out of practice super early. I couldn't believe my good luck! I went downstairs to the locker room and changed into my dark green pants and floral print bodysuit. I liked this outfit and recently got it for my birthday, but I always felt self-conscious wearing it since it was body forming and accentuated my chest and flat stomach.

The other girls were old enough to drive, so they all went home after practice. I looked at my watch and saw that I still had over an hour before Mom would come to pick me up. I thought about calling her to pick me up early, but when I searched in my backpack, I couldn't find any money to call home. All freshmen took enrichment classes, which were several weeklong classes that exposed them to different classes such as art, music, photography, clothing design, and shop classes. I decided to find my next enrichment classroom since I was starting a new class the next week. I looked at my schedule and saw that it was in the fine arts building.

While walking to the fine arts building, I noticed how dark and quiet it was. I noticed that several security lights were burned out, that only one light was working, and that there weren't any stars out. I didn't hear anyone in the gym or walking around outside. I didn't hear anyone talking, and the quietness of the evening was eerie. I don't know if the brisk cool air was making me shiver or if it was from being scared of the dark. Perhaps it was that sixth sense trying to warn me of the danger I would soon encounter. Whatever it was, I remember having goose bumps, and I quickly chided myself for being so scared. I didn't think the door would be open, but since I had so much time to waste, I thought I would go ahead and at least walk over to the fine arts building.

When I got closer to the building, I was surprised to see a dim light coming from the building hallway and that the two doors were wedged open with a floor mat. I thought it was odd that the padlock holding the chain to lock the doors was unlocked and hanging down loose. I looked in through the small glass window on the doors and could barely make out the form of a janitor's cart. *Hmm. The janitor must still be working. He won't mind if I take a look inside and find my classroom.*

As I grabbed the door handle with the hanging chain, I thought, *What luck!* I felt a little guilty sneaking into the building, but since it was jarred open, I thought I'd go in anyway. I opened the door and was going to wait for my eyes to adjust to the dimly lit hallway. I took one step in and instantly was sprayed in my face. My eyes stung, and they felt as if they were on fire. I bent my head down and tried clawing at my eyes, wondering, *What in the world just happened? What is going on? What happened to my eyes? Man, they burn!* Almost immediately, I was pushed from my right side and fell to the ground. I was rolled over and had hard-packed cotton wedges shoved up my nose. My nose felt as if it were on fire, and it made my mouth taste bitter. I still couldn't see because my eyes were still on fire and kept tearing up. My jaw was grabbed, and my mouth was forced open. *What is going on? Yuck, what is that nasty taste? Why is my nose burning? What was just shoved into my nose? Who is doing this to me? Somebody* help *me!*

As I felt and tasted orange juice being poured down my throat, I finally realized who it was. It had to be Coach Carl. He always forced me to drink orange juice with his "secret mix." At this point, I was still completely baffled as to what was going on. My eyes were still stinging, my nose was plugged with cotton, I couldn't see anything, and to make it worse, my clothes were being pulled off. *No! Please don't take my clothes off! Stop it! Someone help me! I don't understand what's going on! I don't hear anyone talking, but I can hear movement like there are several people. I know one must be Coach Carl. Who could the others be? How many are there? Okay, Rachel, focus. Look around and figure out what is going on!*

I tried to get my bearings and figure out what just happened to me. I tried to move and not let them take my clothes off me, but my legs and arms felt as if they weighed a ton. *What is wrong with my legs? Why can't I move? What was in that orange juice? I need to run away! Come on, legs! Get up!*

As hard as I tried, I could not move. I couldn't even begin to try to explain how helpless, frustrated, and terrified I was, knowing that I could not move and that my clothes were being ripped off me. *No, no, no! This can't be happening! Stop! Come on, get up and run!* My eyes didn't sting as much now, but my vision was still foggy. When they finished stripping me, I lay on the cold hallway floor, unable to move. *Please don't look at me! I'm so sorry! What did I do to you? Why are you doing this to me?* I tried to yell and scream, but it only came out as a hoarse whisper and a cough. *So much for having security guards at school! I thought security guards are here to protect us! I need help! Where are you!*

I was dragged a little way down the hall. I was starting to see a little clearer, but I still couldn't move or yell more than a whisper. I was so humiliated as they stood there gawking at my naked body. *Please don't look at me! How am I going to tell my parents? This is so embarrassing! What is going on? Focus, Rachel, focus!* Never in my life have I felt so defeated. Never in my life have I felt so helpless. Never in my life have I been so disgusted with myself.

Even though my vision was still blurred, I could recognize some of my attackers. I saw Coach Carl, Sebastian, a classmate, Shawn, the guy I would later refer to as the "doctor," a guy probably in his twenties, and my homeroom teacher in middle school. Coach Carl stood over me, and with each item of clothing that he took off, I felt sicker and sicker. *How can this be happening to me? It was so important to me to be a virgin until I got married.* But when he stopped before taking off his pants, I had a glimmer of hope. *Maybe he won't rape me. Maybe this is just his sick way of scaring me.* I didn't know what to think. My mind went numb. He just stood there looking at me and nudging me with his foot. *I want to disappear. I wish I could just melt into this floor. Stop looking at me! Get away from me!*

He turned to the "doctor" and said, "How much longer? You know I like a little fight!" The doctor replied, "Shouldn't be much longer. I just gave her a little."

Coach Carl straddled me and slapped me across the face. I was so stunned. *What was that for?* I looked away and tried to see what was going on.

As soon as I looked away, Coach Carl backhanded me across my face. "Look at me! Look at me!" he kept yelling. I looked in his direction, but I still couldn't get my vision to focus. I kept my sight on a blurry spot just past his right shoulder. I felt as if I had left my body and that I was looking down from above. I felt as if it wasn't happening to me but rather to some other girl. I don't know if I was going crazy, but I swear I saw an angel and that the angel held my hand and told me I would be okay.

The angel was an elderly man with a bushy yet well-trimmed white beard. He was a gentle man with gentle sparkling blue eyes. We stood there together, above me being attacked. To this day, I believe that I saw an angel and that I wasn't just going insane. Whatever it was, I felt comforted and believed that I would be okay.

Coach Carl grabbed my head and shook me. "I said to look at me!" he yelled at me. I glanced at him and saw the look of evil in his eyes. So much can be conveyed just through eyes. I knew at that moment that I was at the mercy of his hands and that I would not be able to outsmart him or convince him not to hurt me. I looked at those evil black eyes, and as I did, he slapped me again. "Got some nerve looking at me like that," he sneered. I quickly looked away, but again he got mad at me. He picked up my head and shook me. I couldn't please him. If I looked at him, he got mad. If I didn't look at him, he got mad. What was I supposed to do? His eyes were so evil and malicious-looking that I focused on the bulging vein on his forehead instead. I started to count the pulses in the vein, trying to concentrate on something just to survive the pain and terror. He got up and removed his pants.

"No!" I tried to yell. *I won't let him rape me!* I tried to move my legs so that I could get up and run away. To my amazement, I could actually move! My arms and legs still felt heavy, but at least I could move. When I rolled to my side and began to get up, the twenty-year-old guy pushed me back down. Shawn, Sebastian, and my classmate came over and helped him hold me down. I fought them as hard as I could, but I couldn't get away. I began screaming. *Yes! I could finally scream again!* Despite my fighting, kicking, squirming around and trying so hard to get him off me, Coach Carl raped me. The more I fought him, the more violent he got. Oh, how excruciating the pain! *Why did I wear this bodysuit? I should've known better than to wear such an outfit! I must deserve this.*

I hurt so bad, was tired out from fighting him, and didn't know what to do, so I gave up fighting him and just lay there, looking past him and focusing on the same spot above his shoulder. My angel was still there, with tears in his eyes, and I could feel him holding my hand as I looked down at myself from above. When I looked at that spot, I felt as if I could escape my body and all the pain. I knew it was still me who was being raped, but I could detach the physical and emotional pain from myself. I made my mind and body go numb. I was so sore that I couldn't move.

He told the doctor, "One-eight-nine-eight-six-eight." He then told me to remember that number. *What? You expect me to remember that after what you just did to me? How am I going to remember that number? I can't even think straight! What does that number even mean?* He had me repeat it several times until I could recite it back to him with no mistakes.

Coach Carl grabbed my ponytail and pulled me up so that I was standing up. My legs trembled, and my whole body was weak from pain and fear. Shawn pushed me up against the lockers and held me there as he yelled at me to kiss him. I would never kiss him! He punched me several times and then kissed me all over my face and neck. Feeling his kisses made me nauseated. I hated how he kissed me and knowing I couldn't do anything about it. He let go of me, so I made a dash for the door at the end of the hallway. I only got a few steps before Shawn tackled me and the others held me to the ground. Shawn raped me, and as he was getting off of me, he spit in my face and smirked, "How'd you like that?"

I just want to die. Why is this happening to me? What did I do to them? Please stop. Please go away!

As I was trying to hide my body as much as possible, the whole group surrounded me and began making crude comments about me and cheering each other on. *How gross and perverted can you be? You guys are monsters! What are you on? Are you high? What's wrong with you? What's wrong with me? Why didn't I walk home after practice? Why can't I get away? Why don't I yell more? Why can't I scream louder? I don't understand. I don't understand what is going on! Help!* I was forced into standing as they pushed me from one guy to the next. As I was pushed and tumbled around their circle, the guys would grab my body, spit on me, and slap me. Then they started taking turns doing whatever they wanted to do to me. *I can't do this any longer! It hurts so bad! Please stop! God, just please let me die! I'm so ashamed! What's wrong with me? What's wrong with you, Sebastian? You were always so nice to me! I'm so sorry for flirting with you! I'm so sorry! You were my friend—why are you hurting me like this? This isn't like you! I'm so sorry!* I was so disgusted, humiliated, and terrified that I threw up on the floor. Coach Carl shoved my face into the vomit and demanded that I lick it up. I was so humiliated. He kept telling me that I was nothing but garbage, a messed-up dirty girl, that my parents would be so disappointed with me, and that I probably wouldn't be allowed in church for sinning so terribly. They said that if I told anyone what happened tonight, they would do this to my little sister, Abigail.

As my face was shoved into the vomit, all I could think of was begging God to let me die. *I have to keep Abigail safe! I can't let these monsters go near her! I'm such a screwup! How can I ever face my parents after this? How can I ever take a step into church? How can God ever forgive me? How can I put this behind me and go on with my life? How can I ever go back to school and see these monsters every day? I can't believe this just happened. This must be a nightmare—this can't be true! God, I'm begging you, please let me die!* All the way to the depths of my soul, I was torn and damaged. My life as I knew it was dead.

They pulled over the janitor's cleaning cart and made me clean up the mess on the floor. They left me all alone in the dim, cold, lonely hallway. I was in such a daze as I gathered up my clothes and tried to figure out what to do next. I couldn't find my bra, underwear, or bodysuit, so I went back into the locker room and quickly cleaned up and changed into my practice clothes. I was still bleeding from some cuts and scratches, and I didn't have any underwear, so I packed a wad of toilet paper between my legs. I was still in a daze as I went outside for Mom to pick me up. I saw her parked, waiting for me. I quickly opened the passenger side door and slid in, closed the door, and locked the door. Thank goodness it was dark outside—Mom wouldn't be able to see my face.

I was still in such shock that I don't remember much about that car ride home. I just remember Mom talking nonstop about how excited she was about having our cousins from Wyoming join us for Christmas. As soon as we got home, I raced up the stairs to the bathroom and took an extra long hot shower. I couldn't get into that shower quickly enough. I was so eager to wash away all the evil that was done to me.

No matter how hard I scrubbed myself with the nailbrush, I couldn't get the "badness" to disappear. I remember standing under the scalding hot water and watching the water by my feet turning pink from the blood trickling down my thighs. The pink water mesmerized me, and I could feel myself leaving my body.

I didn't return to my body until I heard Mom pounding on the door, telling me to hurry up and not to use so much hot water since my little brother, Ben, still had to take a bath. I brushed my teeth until my mouth was bleeding. No matter how hard I brushed my teeth, my tongue, and the inside of my mouth, I couldn't get rid of the nasty taste. I got dressed and hurried out the bathroom. I quickly went to my bedroom. While hurrying down the hallway to my bedroom, I could hear Christmas music and my family having a great time decorating the Christmas tree. I instantly got mad since they were all singing Christmas songs and laughing with joy while here I was in such pain. From that night on, I became withdrawn and isolated myself from my family.

I'm not good enough to belong to the family. I'm too big of a sinner. I'm the black sheep of the family, and I have to punish myself for being so bad. I was so disappointed with myself. I had always been able to out-smart people and get myself out of sticky situations. I prided myself that I never needed help. *Now what do I do? What a mess I got myself into!*

Chapter 8

The day after

The next day, I convinced my mom that I was too tired to go to school. She let me sleep in, and I didn't go to school until third hour. I put extra makeup on to cover some bruises on my face, went to school, and forced myself to act like nothing happened. I wouldn't allow myself to even think about what happened. I pushed it out of my memory and locked it in a box far, far away from my conscious memory. This all worked until I went to math class. I sat down at my desk and began talking to my friend Amanda. As we were talking, the classmate that raped me walked into the classroom.

As soon as I saw him, I got sick to my stomach, stopped talking, and began to tremble. I was so white and shaking that Amanda asked me what was wrong and said that I looked like I just saw a ghost. Without answering her, I dashed out the door and ran right into my math teacher. I quickly explained that I was sick and ran up the path to the main school building. Just as I got to the doors, I leaned over the stair railing and threw up. I held onto the railing for support and stood there trembling, not knowing what to do. I eventually stopped trembling and hid from the security guards.

I was able to get calm once again, and I went to my next class, Spanish. I sat down and talked to Travis. What a nice, thoughtful friend. Talking to Travis was like a breath of fresh air. As the bell rang for class to begin, Travis slid out of the seat next to me and went to his desk, which was two seats in front of me. Just as Senora Sanchez was about to close the door and begin class, Sebastian slid in and took his seat right in front of me.

In disbelief, I just watched him sit down. He turned around, smiled at me, and smirked. "How'd you like last night?" My heart began to beat harder and faster, making me shaky. I don't remember anything about Spanish class that day. I just kept looking at the back of Sebastian's head, trying to lose myself by glaring at his dark black glossy hair. *I have to push down the memory of last night. I just have to! Stay calm. Nothing really happened. It was just a bad dream or a bad movie. Come on—be strong!*

As soon as the bell rang, I jumped up and ran out of the classroom. Travis yelled at me to stop and to wait for him, but I just wanted to get out of there—as far away from Sebastian as I could. Travis caught up with me and asked me what was wrong. I couldn't tell him. I liked Travis, and I didn't want anything to ruin our friendship. I didn't want him to think I was making things up to get his attention. Plus, I kept telling myself that it didn't happen to me anyway. I was just going crazy. I didn't even know why I was so scared. *What is wrong with me? Why am I so scared of Sebastian? Why does he make me feel sick?* I didn't remember being raped; I just remembered being terrified of last night. Talk about feeling crazy—terrified to death but not even knowing why! I now realize that I was too traumatized and that I had blocked out the memory of being raped. The brain is amazing, and I had learned how to dissociate in order to survive.

On my way to the locker room to change for my basketball game, a guy I had never seen before came up to me and shoved a plastic Baggie into my hand. I looked at the Baggie and saw several white pills. He said I looked stressed and that I should take some to help me relax. I looked at the Baggie and thought, *No way! I would never take drugs!*

The boy took off down the hall. *What am I going to do with this Baggie of drugs? I don't want the security guards to catch me with drugs!* I quickly stuffed the Baggie into my pants pocket and raced down to the locker room to get dressed for the game. I looked around the locker room and noticed I was the first one there. I went to my locker but couldn't undo the lock since I was trembling and not able to focus on the numbers on the lock. I began to panic and hyperventilate. *Come on, Rachel, calm down. Breathe. Relax.* I put my hand in my pocket, took out the Baggie, studied it, and looked around as I rolled the pills between my fingers. *Why not? Yeah, I'm stressed out. I need to relax and get this out of my mind!* I opened the Baggie and took two pills. I put the rest in my locker under some clothes on the top shelf. As the other girls began to fill up the locker room and the laughter and talking got louder and louder, I could feel myself drift away.

I could feel myself beginning to relax as I focused on the thumping of the loud rap music being played in the gym upstairs. I knew some of the other girls on JV were talking to me, but I wasn't listening to them. I was so focused on the music that I didn't even hear or notice anything else. I felt as if I were walking on a cloud in a dreamlike motion. *This is so much better! Those were good pills! Is this what it's like being on drugs? I'll have to be careful—I don't want to end up being a druggie!* Once the JV team and I got upstairs and started warming up, I was a little more with it and able to play ball. I soon forgot about all my worries and just lost myself in the music and the excitement of playing the game.

During the second quarter, I went up for a rebound and twisted my ankle. As my ankle twisted. I fell to the ground in pain and hobbled over to the bench with the rest of the team. As soon as I sat down, I took off my sock and shoe and saw that my ankle was swollen. Gianna, the assistant for JV, gave me a bag of ice to put on my ankle. As I was holding the ice on my ankle and watching the game, I suddenly feel someone grabbing my shoulders and massaging them too forcefully. Before I could even turn around, I could smell him. I knew who it was. It was Shawn. I instantly felt as if my body turned into ice. I began to shiver. *No! No! No! Get away from me, you monster!*

He grabbed my shoulders and the back of my neck and whispered, "Don't let the team down. You have to be loyal. We're watching you." With that, he got up and left. I turned to watch him leave, looking at him in disbelief and in fear.

Out of the corner of my eye, I saw my mom coming over to me. I could tell she was surprised that I wasn't in the game. When she got over to me, she asked why I wasn't playing. I told her I hurt my ankle and that it hurt too much to play. It was soon halftime, so she quickly talked to Alex and said that she was going to take me to the doctor and get my ankle checked out. While on the way to the doctor, Mom interrogated me about that "cute, nice boy" who was massaging my neck and shoulders. *What! How can you say that, Mom?* I almost choked as she said, "nice boy." As she went on and on about the "nice boy being so attentive to me" and being so helpful, I just kept thinking she had no clue! *Ahhh! Just shut up, Mom! You don't know what you're talking about! Seriously, stop talking about him!* I wanted to yell at her to just stop talking and not to call him a nice boy. I was so irritated with her. She was so clueless, and she wouldn't understand since she already had her mind made up. Instead of yelling at her, as I so badly wanted to do, I quietly told her that it was Shawn. It disgusted me seeing her think it was so nice that I was interested in guys and that I had such a "nice, attentive guy friend."

The doctor told me that I had a pretty severe sprain and that I would need to walk on crutches and wear an Aircast. Mom was going to take me home, but I insisted on going back to the game. I kept thinking of Shawn's threat that I need to be loyal and that they were always watching me. I knew Coach Carl would be furious with me since I was expected to play for the varsity game since two other girls were sick and not able to play. At first, Mom wasn't going to let me go back to the game, but I became so irrational and upset about not being there and said that I needed to be loyal to the team that she finally gave in and dropped me off at school, promising me she'd be back to pick me up after the girls' varsity game.

I hobbled out of the car and went in the gym. I saw that the boys' JV game was just about to end and that the girls' varsity team was starting to congregate together by the stairs. I didn't have crutches yet, but I was in my Aircast, and I limped over to the team. Coach Carl saw that I was still in my JV uniform and yelled at me to change. I tried to explain to him that I didn't need to change since I would just sit on the bench with my warm-up clothes on and watch the team play. He wouldn't even listen. He just yelled at me again and told me to go downstairs and change. He said I didn't have a choice; I had to play tonight.

As I was going down the stairs to the locker room, he grabbed me and walked me to the trainer's room. He closed the door, locked it, gave me a pill, and forced me to drink orange juice. He raised his arm as if he was going to strike me, but I was saved by a knock on the door. He lowered his arm, hissing at me to be loyal to the team and not to talk back to him. He opened the door, and Alex was there. Alex looked at me with a questioning look as Coach Carl told him I was going to play. Alex asked if I was okay to play and wanted to know what the doctor told me, but I didn't even have a chance to tell him. Coach Carl said I just rolled it and that I was fine and needed to suck it up for the team. Then he pushed me out of the room and had me get ready for the game.

During warm-ups, I tried so hard not to put much weight on my ankle and not to wince every time I took a step. I knew that if I showed my pain or my weakness, Coach Carl would only make it worse for me. I had to stop thinking about it. I had to make myself numb. I had to detach myself from reality. It must have worked, for I played most of the game. I don't remember playing the game, but my ankle remembered. It was extremely swollen, sore, and black and blue.

Chapter 9

Christmas break

My aunt Gina, uncle Martin, and my cousins Keith, Allison, and Eric visited us for two weeks over Christmas break. My whole family looked forward to this since we didn't get to see them very often since we lived in different states. I loved being on vacation. I was safe from Coach Carl and Shawn. I could enjoy myself and actually have fun.

Allison, my sister Abigail, and I all slept in my room, and we enjoyed staying up late at night and having girl talk. When Abigail would fall asleep, Allison and I would talk about boyfriends and such. She noticed that I had a bump on my forehead and asked me what it was from. I tried to ignore her question and change the subject, but she kept asking me about it. I began telling her that there was this guy at school who was harassing me and quite possessive of me. I told her how he would get mad at me for talking to any other guy and that he had pushed me into the locker and that was how I got the bump. I told her that he sometimes tried to touch me even though I didn't want him to. I tried to downplay the whole situation and said that it was fine now. Our conversation died down, and I pretended I was asleep. Allison snuck out of my room and went to the living room to talk to my older brother, Luke, about our conversation.

Once she was out of the room, I quietly snuck out behind her and went down the hallway. I sat on the steps with my back pushed up against the warm brick fireplace, listening carefully to what Luke and

Allison were talking about. At first, all I could hear was the rocking chair moving back and forth. Allison must have gotten Luke's attention. He'd been wearing headphones and listening to music as he rocked. The rocking slowed down, and I could hear Allison asking Luke if he or my parents knew anything about the boy who was bothering me. Luke didn't say anything, and Allison continued telling him that I was being sexually harassed at school. Luke laughed and said that I was a big flirt at school and probably just gave some boy the wrong idea. He said she didn't need to worry since I was able to take care of myself. He went on to tell her how aggressive I was at soccer and basketball and that if anyone crossed paths with me, that person had better watch out. He went on about how I flirted with his friends and said that I was naive about boyfriends. I couldn't take it any longer. *My own brother was saying that I asked for it? He wasn't going to protect me? Didn't he believe me?* I got up and ran down the hall back to my room. Allison and Luke heard me, and Allison came back to my room.

I was so mad at myself for telling her. No, I didn't tell her much, but I still felt as if I told way too much. I was angry with her for telling Luke since she promised me she wouldn't tell anyone. As angry as I was, I sort of felt relieved. I felt relieved that I let some of my horrible secret out. However, with Luke's response, I realized that Coach Carl was right: no one would believe me. *If my own brother doesn't believe me, why would anyone else? I'll just have to be more careful about hiding my bruises and pain. I cannot tell anyone!*

Wednesday, January 5, 1994

We were playing at home, and it was my first game back without crutches! I was feeling so relieved to be without them. *Maybe I wouldn't be such an easy target!* Once school was back in session, Shawn kept coming up to me, putting his arm around my neck, and pushing me against the lockers. He kept telling people we were married and kept trying to kiss me. One day he whispered in my ear that I'd better watch out because I was going to get it during the boys' JV game that night. Apparently, other people knew this also, for several of the other girls on the team told me to be careful that night since they heard Shawn had a plan for me. I didn't know what "it" was or what his plan was, so I decided it was only a threat and that he wasn't serious. I pushed his threat out of my mind and didn't give it another thought.

I played okay for the JV game, but by the time the game was over, my ankle was throbbing. I was going to put some ice on it between games, so I started to go to the trainer's room. I decided to get a quick drink of water first, and I stopped at the water fountain just outside the trainer's room. I was getting a drink when Shawn came up behind me and grabbed my ponytail. He banged my head against the back of the white porcelain water fountain and told me to come downstairs with him now. *Now what did I do?* I asked myself.

I felt I had no choice, so I started going down the stairs. My ankle was hurting, so I went down slowly, one step at a time, pausing after every step. Shawn got impatient with me and pushed me. I tripped and fell down the last two cement steps. While I was on the cold cement floor, I looked up and saw how evil Shawn looked. Something in his eyes told me that tonight would be different. *I need to get out of here! I need to get away from him! Help!* I got scared and tried to get out the door. Before I could get outside, Shawn caught me and threw me down the next few steps to the landing by the lower gym. He was instantly on top of me and slammed my head into the floor, hissing at me to stop making so much noise. He held his knife to my side, its tip pricking me. I struggled and tried to get away. I rolled to my right side just as Shawn raised his knife and stabbed my left shoulder. He held me down as he put white bandage tape over my mouth and knife wound.

He dragged me into the lower gym, which was used for wrestling practices. Coach Carl was in there, and he had me take off my shoes and socks so that he could look at my ankle. I thought he was actually going to be nice since he held a bag of ice and seemed to care about my ankle. He was bent over me looking at my ankle and holding the bag of ice as if he were going to put it on my ankle. Coach Carl touched it and asked me if it hurt. I nodded. He immediately hit me across my face with the bag of ice. I was stunned since I didn't even see it coming. *What did I do now?*

He told Shawn to get some orange juice. As Shawn left, Coach Carl grabbed my arms behind my back and pushed me against the gym wall. He slid me down so that I was lying on my stomach, arms still held back. He got on top of me and straddled me. He let go of my arms, but I was still pinned down. He used my long white sock to blindfold me. He tied it so tight; it felt as if the corners of my eyes were torn.

Shawn returned with the orange juice. I was turned over onto my back, had the tape ripped off my mouth, and was forced to drink it. Coach Carl grabbed my wrists behind my back again and forced me to walk. I didn't even try to yell; I knew it was pointless and would only get me in more trouble. I hate to admit it, but they broke me. They broke my spirit to fight and to stand up for myself. They broke my sense of who I was. They broke my strong will. They broke me down to be a walking dummy to which they could do anything they wanted.

No, I was never a prisoner behind bars or even held captive with any physical barriers, but I was still a prisoner. I was *their* prisoner. They had me so scared, so brainwashed, and so broken down that I was their prisoner in a horrible, daunting never-ending nightmare. I often beat myself up for not running away from their entrapments and never telling my parents or asking for help. No, I did not have any physical barriers, but after the daily threats, the daily blackmail, the daily beatings, the daily humiliation, and constantly being on guard and being terrified, in my mind, I *was* behind bars. I was trapped and had no way to escape. I had to do what they said in order to survive. One thing I would not let them take away from me was the desire to persevere through this valley of darkness.

I tripped and fell face-first onto a wrestling mat. I was told to get up. I was pushed ahead a little more and told to climb over the rolled-up mats. I began to feel for the rolled-up mat so I could climb over it, but then I was pushed over a mat and landed on my face on another mat laid out on the gym floor. I was on my stomach, and someone had his knee pressed up against my back, pinning me down. I was stripped of my uniform shorts and was told to say my number.

As I was saying one-eight-nine-eight-six-eight, my arms were pulled above me, my wrists were taped together, and my ankles were taped together so that I could only move my ankles a little distance apart. Someone got on top of me. I didn't even try to fight him. I just lay there and tried to do what he wanted. At one point, the sock blindfold moved a little so I could just see a little out of the corner of my left eye. I first saw a bright light, which blinded me. As my eyes adjusted, I could see it was coming from a video camera. I saw the blinking red light indicating I was being videotaped. I couldn't see who was videotaping. I saw the blue and red mats rolled up all around us. I saw I was lying on a blue mat. I saw the legs of my rapist: muscular white legs with lots of dark hair. I saw several pairs of people's shoes and various pant legs. I saw that it was pitch black in the gym, except for the blinding video camera light. I saw my rapist's right arm. It had a tattoo that was a dark color. The tattoo wasn't a picture of anything—just some kind of swirly design.

I kept thinking, *Just hurry up and get it done already!* I blocked everything out. I blocked out the flashing red light and the fact that several people were watching me get raped and not helping me. I blocked out his awful grunting noises and that I felt like a rag doll being thrown all over while my hands and feet were bound. I blocked out his heavy breathing and alcohol breath. I blocked out the overwhelming smell of sweat coming from the wrestling mat. Instead, I focused on making me leave this body. I couldn't take it anymore. I had to leave. I physically couldn't, so I had to mentally. In order to survive and stay sane, I had to detach myself from this torment. I was so glad that my homeroom teacher taught me the secret of how to survive torture! It worked. I was able to leave.

The next thing I knew, I heard the gym door slam. I jerked to attention and noticed I wasn't bound anymore and that my blindfold was off. I sat there for a while, letting my eyes adjust to the darkness. I felt with my hands that my clothes were in a pile next to me. As I got dressed in the darkness, the only light coming from the green neon exit signs, I noticed that my left ankle had sticky liquid on it. I got dressed except for my socks and shoes. I opened the gym door and saw Coach Carl's office. The light was on. *Oh no! Not again! Just leave me alone!* When the light was on, it meant that I had an "assignment." I hated seeing that light on. *Maybe I just had my "assignment" and I can just go play the next game. Maybe I was done for the night.*

Seeing the clock through the glass windows of his office, I realized that I still had a while before the varsity game began. I went to the locker room to change into my varsity uniform. I saw that my left ankle was cut and bleeding. As I was at my locker, I heard the door open. I thought it might be Tamika since she began to play for both JV and varsity too. I called out to her. No answer. I was about to put on my uniform shirt when I heard Coach Carl and the doctor talking.

I froze. I willed myself to melt into the ground, but it didn't work. I turned and saw them standing at the end of the aisle. I froze. I couldn't even move to run away. I instantly turned into their little lifeless robot, waiting to do as they beckoned. *I'm so mad at myself! Why do I keep doing this? Why don't I fight them anymore? What's wrong with me? Help! Someone please help me!*

I was told to lie down on the bench. I did. *What are they going to do to me now? Can't they just leave me alone? What did I do to deserve this? What is wrong with me? Why do they hate me so much? How can they be so evil? I'm so confused. I don't understand them. How can this keep happening to me? How can I keep hiding my pain and pretending that everything is fine?*

The doctor tended to my wound on my shoulder and took out a syringe from his black duffel bag. He stuck the syringe into the side of my neck. My body instantly became numb. My arms went limp. My legs went limp. I couldn't move. *Help! Help me! Somebody help! No! Please don't hurt me! Please stop!* They carried me to the far back room to the showers. I only had on my uniform shorts, underwear, and sports bra, but these were then removed. Shawn, "video guy," my homeroom teacher from middle school, Detective Clark, and Sebastian were there waiting for us. My homeroom teacher told me to say my number and added that I was now "Rosalita." He kept asking who I was, until I told him I was Rosalita. He informed me that I had a huge debt that I needed to pay off. I had no idea what he was talking about. He showed me black-and-white photographs of me partying on a yacht and drinking alcohol the summer after I came home from Mexico. With a heavy heart and complete dread, my mind instantly went back to that night on the yacht:

I had always been a good girl, but while in Mexico, I rebelled a little and lived vicariously through my Spanish class persona, Rosalita.

A few days after our trip, we all went to my friend Kerri's house to exchange pictures and talk about our trip and funny memories. While at her house, Sebastian's brother, Juan, called to let Sebastian know he was coming to pick him up. When Juan got to Kerri's house, he invited all of us to come to a party on his friend's yacht. We decided to go. We couldn't all fit in Juan's car, so he called his friend to help drive some of us there. Sebastian, Kerri, Erin, Tamara, and I all squeezed into Juan's car. Juan squealed out of the driveway and drove to the yacht extremely fast, having fun jerking the wheel so that we all bumped into each other and into the window. I was feeling nervous but a little excited to go to my first high school party with no parents.

The road to the marina was curvy and wound down the bluff. It was dark outside; Juan was driving like a lunatic and smoking weed. I was sitting between Sebastian and Tamara, and whenever Juan jerked the wheel or went around a bend, I would slam into Sebastian. Sebastian thought this was great fun and enjoyed the opportunity to grab me and touch me. I was getting mad at him for touching me, and I was terrified that we were going to drive off the side of the bluff. I wasn't having any fun anymore. I was terrified for my life!

We finally parked and got to the marina. I didn't want to be a party pooper, so I caved into peer pressure and climbed aboard the largest, most beautiful yacht I had ever seen. It was so large that it almost took up the entire length of the dock. We climbed aboard and entered the scene of a crazy party. High school kids were drinking alcohol, smoking pot, dancing, making out, playing cards, and being super loud. I had never witnessed such a party before, and I was overwhelmed and scared. I didn't know what to do. I felt way out of my element.

I thought I would go play cards since that seemed innocent enough. I sat down at the table, and I was soon trapped on the bench seat between Sebastian and his brother. There were several other students at the table, and we played card games. I enjoy playing cards, and I get quite competitive. I began to enjoy myself and was more relaxed. As the game went on, I got thirsty so I asked for a drink. Sebastian got me what I thought was Pepsi. I took a sip and asked what it was. He said it was just soda and that I didn't have to worry since I could trust him. We continued playing cards, and I downed my entire drink. Sebastian got me another drink. Before long, I was feeling quite comfortable and very relaxed. I was laughing a lot and thought everything was hilarious. I didn't realize it, but Sebastian had spiked my drink; I was getting drunk. I'm sure the pot smoke from Juan and his friends wasn't helping anything either.

I don't remember much about that night, but I know that I had a hangover the next morning. I don't remember how we all got back to Kerri's house. I don't remember all that happened that night. After that night, I vowed that I'd never drink alcohol again ...

Seeing those pictures made me feel sick. I was so ashamed. I felt so horrible that I had kept that a secret from my parents and that I would be so stupid to go to a party and get drunk. I couldn't believe I could be so stupid and be so provocative. I couldn't believe that they had pictures of me back then. *When did they start following me? How did they know that my Spanish name in middle school was Rosalita and that Rosalita was a party girl who was sexual and flirtatious? Stacy didn't go to Mexico with us ... How did Detective Clark know about Mexico? Shoot! Now he has even more dirt on me!*

I thought those pictures were bad enough, but then I saw the next pictures that Detective Clark showed me. He had pictures of me being raped by Shawn and other guys that I didn't even know. I looked away, but Detective Clark shoved them in my face and forced me to look at them. However, just by looking at the pictures, the person looking at the pictures would have no idea of the horror I went through or how I was being forced to lie there and be raped. Just looking at the pictures, I appeared to be a willing participant in sex. Looking at the pictures made me want to vomit. They brought back so many horrible, painful memories. I felt so dirty. *Maybe I was just a dirty little prostitute. Maybe I'm garbage. Maybe I'm too bad to go to church. What would my parents think and say?* I was doing such a good job of stuffing those memories into a locked box in the farthest corner of my conscious brain until now. After seeing those pictures, I couldn't deny it. I really *was* raped. This really did happen to me. Now what was I going to do?

My homeroom teacher kept talking about the huge debt I owed them; I had no idea what debt he was even talking about. He threatened me that if I didn't pay it off, they would send these pictures to my parents. He asked me, "What do you think your parents would think if they saw these pictures? They would never believe you that you were raped. These pictures show just how dirty you are! Imagine how they would feel when they got to the mailbox, opened the envelope, and took out these pictures. Imagine the shock and horror they would feel! Imagine how disappointed and angry they would be with you! You're lucky that we're even giving you a chance to pay it off. Maybe we should change our minds and just send these pictures anyway!"

Detective Clark joined in by saying, "Don't even think about telling anyone. Who would they believe—a dirty little prostitute like you or a respected detective like me? I know how to make evidence disappear and how to frame you! Do you want to be the next girl in my crime scene photos? You're nothing but a crazy messed-up girl. You're nothing!"

I was so humiliated and ashamed. *He's right … I'm nothing. Who would believe me? I messed up way too much … How do I even start to dig myself out of this deep hole I created? I'm so ashamed. I deserve this. I'm so stupid.* I would never want my parents to see such pictures of me! I quietly asked what I needed to do to pay off the debt.

He confidently replied that I would need to do anything and everything they told me to do. I was worried what they had in mind for me to do, so I hesitated with my answer. He started to tell Shawn my address, and Shawn wrote my address on the large manila folder holding pictures of my horrible secret. *No! I can't let Mom and Dad see how dirty I am! I can't disappoint them!* I reluctantly agreed to do what they said. My homeroom teacher made me repeat my answer until he had it on tape: "I agree." I would forever regret saying those words. *Now what's going to happen? I really don't want to do anything with them … but what else can I say or do? What a mess! Please don't hurt me! Please forgive me, God!*

The doctor gave Coach Carl some tape, and they taped my hands together at the wrists. I thought this was pointless since I still couldn't move. Not being able to move from the shot in my neck was frustrating, but now that I was bound, I was even more scared and angry. *I hate being tied down. I hate not being able to move. I hate not being able to fight. Get away from me! Stop!* I was told to smile and to look as if I were enjoying being touched. I couldn't believe it! *How am I supposed to smile when you're doing this to me? Do you really think I enjoy this?* Dumbfounded, I just looked at them. Coach Carl got mad at me and backhanded me across the face. I gave them a little smile. They said it wasn't good enough and that I needed to do a real smile. Do you realize how difficult it is to do a real smile when your whole body and mind are telling you this is wrong?

Shawn got his knife out and pressed it against my throat. He was so angry and irrational, and I was afraid that he would slice my throat on accident. I tried to lie there as still as possible so that I wouldn't jerk his hand with the knife. *Oh no! He's going to kill me! Please stop! Okay, okay, okay … I'll do anything you say!* He took the knife blade and gently traced from my lips up my cheek to where he wanted my smile to end. He returned the blade to my throat and told me to smile. I tried to smile the way he wanted me to, but I guess it wasn't good enough for he pressed the blade deeper. *I can't do this! Come on, Rachel, smile! Calm down and don't move—don't make him slice your throat! I'm so scared. He's going to kill me!*

I knew I wouldn't be able to smile the way they wanted me to. I knew I wouldn't be able to please them. I was so terrified of having my throat sliced; I needed to do something in order to survive. I blocked everything out and focused on the little spots on the gray ceiling. I eventually learned how to smile correctly for them, and I made myself turn into Rosalita.

There was loud music playing from the gym upstairs, and I lost myself while listening to the heavy thumps of the bass and from the game being played. Sebastian started to rape me, and I couldn't get him off. I tried so hard to roll to my side, but it was no use. I couldn't get free. While struggling, I noticed the little red blinking light. I was being videotaped again. They kept telling me to smile. I just wanted him to be done, so I did as they said. I smiled, but it was a lifeless smile. I was dead inside.

I didn't even know who I had become. Most of the time, I didn't even feel as if I were present. I was under so much pressure and stress, and I kept pushing everything out of my memory. I felt I was constantly living a dream, a horrible nightmare that I could never wake up from. My happy, carefree life as I knew it was dead. All my dreams of being a virgin until marriage were dead. All my dreams of having a good time in high school were dead. All my dreams of dating and falling in love with a nice guy were dead.

While I was being raped by Sebastian, Shawn and Coach Carl began to undress. I couldn't believe it. *Can't they just leave me alone? What all do I have to do for them? I am still sore from before … I need a break! Just please leave me alone!* I either blacked out from the pain or was so successful in blocking everything out that the next thing I remember is having the shower on me and Coach Carl saying that I needed to be upstairs to play in fifteen minutes. He threw me an envelope as he walked away whistling. I scrubbed my body, threw the condom wrappers away, dried off, and got dressed in my varsity uniform. I looked inside the envelope and saw several twenty dollar bills. I felt sick. *Am I now a real prostitute?* I threw the envelope of money onto Coach Carl's desk in his office. *I would never take his awful dirty money! He will not make me believe I am a prostitute! I will never lower myself to the point of where I will take his money. What did I just do? What did I get myself into? How can I make this stop? How can I keep going on like this? Doesn't anyone know that I'm dying inside and need help?*

I went upstairs to get ready for warm-ups, but I was late and there were only a few more minutes left for warm-ups before the game would begin. I tried to run and play, but I was so sore I couldn't move. I was forced to drink orange juice, but I was still in such excruciating pain. I begged Coach Carl to just let me sit this game out since I was in such pain. He was furious with me and kept saying how I needed to be loyal to the team. I tried so hard to play, but it was obvious that I just couldn't. I was allowed to sit on the bench during the game.

Mom came a little after the game began. I saw her enter the gym and search for me on the basketball court. Once she noticed that I wasn't playing, I saw her hustle over to the bleachers with a questioning look on her face. She came over by me and was surprised that I wasn't playing. I told her my ankle hurt too much and that I had an awful headache. I knew I would get in trouble with Coach Carl, but I just wanted to get out of there. Thankfully, he didn't argue with me and Mom took me home.

I felt so alone. The loneliness was worse than the physical pain I endured. I was in such torment; I was hurting so bad—inside and outside—and I couldn't tell anyone. The more lonely and hurt I felt, the more silent I had to be. No one heard my desperate silent cries for help. No one heard or saw my silent tearless crying at night as I lay curled up into a tight ball wishing I could end it all. I was hurting so much. I needed help, but I couldn't ask for it. I couldn't let anyone even know that I was hurting. I was dying inside, and nobody knew it. I was all alone. That loneliness almost killed me. I became suicidal. I never wanted to kill myself, but I didn't know how else to live with this immense pain. I didn't know how to end this horrible cycle. The physical and emotional pain was so constant that I eventually couldn't feel the pain anymore. It came close to killing my spirit …

Chapter 10

I felt as if I couldn't tell anyone or let anyone know that I was hurting, but I secretly began to write about my pain via poems in my notebook. One of the poems that I wrote in early January:

Fear

She cringes in a lonely corner,
Afraid of that hand
Above in the air.
Many a time that
Hand has hurt her.
She searches to find
Someone who cares,
Her silent screams ringing
Out into the night.
Silent stinging tears
Want so desperately to roll
Down her face,
But they mustn't.
She doesn't have
Enough strength to fight.
She reaches out for
Gentle arms to embrace,
But all that's there
Is the cold air.

> *Her safe world has*
> *Now been shattered,*
> *And she cries alone,*
> *Thinking nobody cares.*

January 8, 1994

Well, I'm starting a journal tonight. Maybe when I write about all my problems, I'll feel better. I hate Shawn. He keeps telling me to get hurt so that he can kiss it better. He keeps asking if I like him, and I keep telling him I never did and never will. Yesterday he said that I could at least start to like him. Tamika heard him and asked what we could start. He said we could start to do "it." His hand was going up my leg, and Tamika and I told him to stop. He said he was only kidding … Yeah, right. He kept telling me that I couldn't leave him because he had a crush on me and that he would make me like him. I can't get away from him!

Yesterday in basketball practice, the coaches made me feel good by cheering for me. At the end of practice, we broke up into groups and shot three-point shots. In one minute, I got nine three-pointers!

January 11, 1994

A lot has happened since the last time I wrote in here. Last night I opened up to the first person—Travis—about what happened on the bus ride home on December 10. Travis and I talked for a long time. I don't know how he does it, but he is always able to get me to tell him everything on my mind and cheer me up. He said it was a Helping Friend rule that for problems like this, he would have to let Regina know. He can do whatever he needs to do, but I'm not going to go in to see any counselor. Well, everything was fine until Travis saw me at the end of lunch. He said I really needed to go with him to Regina's office. I started walking with him, but when I saw Amanda, I left Travis and walked with her. I was too nervous to talk to Regina, and I kept leaving Travis. Then the bell rang and I went to class.

Soon after class started, an office TA came in with a request to report slip. The slip was for me to see the assistant principal! Everyone in class said, "Oooh, Rachel. What did you do?" When I got there, the assistant principal was busy, so I just stood there trying to act calm, even though I really felt like bursting. She was finally ready to talk to me, but I just sat there saying nothing, which got her super mad, and she sent me to talk to Regina. Regina is much nicer and easier to talk to. She said she would have to call my parents, but I asked if Luke could come before she called. It was helpful having Luke with me, and we promised we would tell Mom and Dad. When we got home, Mom asked why we were home so early. I went to my room, and Luke told Mom while I took a nap. This was my first sleep for a couple of days, and it felt so nice! I feel so relieved now that my parents know. I don't know why I was stressing so much about telling them. I'm so glad this is all going to end!

I was spending more and more time with my good friend Travis. I was really beginning to like him, maybe more than just as a friend. We spent many hours talking on the phone, writing notes during Spanish class, and talking in the hall between classes. Even though Shawn would harass me even more when I was around Travis, I still felt safe being with him. Travis always treated me with respect and made me feel like the real Rachel. When I was with Travis, I could forget all the pain I was in. I felt normal around Travis ... I could forget the mess I was involved in. He saw me for who I was, not the dirty, worthless girl I often felt like.

A few times, Travis saw me being hit and pushed down the stairs by Shawn and being harassed by Sebastian. He was extremely concerned and kept asking me what was going on. I kept saying that everything was fine and not to worry about me. *I can't let Travis know what is going on! I can't let him know how dirty I am!*

Despite my nonchalant answers and dismissing his concerns, Travis knew it was more than just the harassment. He kept talking to me and asking me what was going on. Knowing that he was a "Helping Friend," a school program that taught select students how to be peer counselors, I knew I could trust him. Despite that, I kept testing him by saying just a little and gauging how he responded. He never blamed me or overreacted to what I told him, so I slowly began to tell him what was going on between Shawn, Sebastian, and me. We began writing notes back and forth, and I eventually told him that they were touching me and scaring me. He insisted that I talk to the school nurse, Regina.

I grudgingly went to her office. I just sat there and stared at her. I was furious with Travis for betraying my trust, but he explained that such things need to be reported. After staring Regina down for over an hour, I finally told her that I was being sexually harassed by Shawn. I told her of the incident on the bus ride back home from a game. I was shaking with fear while I sat in the chair and talked. Since I was careful not to say too much, I'm sure I wasn't making much sense. She could tell I was scared, and she was very understanding and sincere. I decided I liked her and could trust her. I told her I wanted to talk to my brother Luke, so she had him sent to her office. Luke and I talked and decided we would skip basketball and swimming practice and go home to tell Mom and Dad. Luke was supportive and understanding as he drove me home.

When we got home, Mom and Dad were surprised to see us home so early. They first looked surprised, and then they got that worried look on their faces. I was too embarrassed to talk to them about Shawn, so I ran up the steps and into my room. I flopped down on my bed and just cried. I didn't cry out loud, but I allowed the tears to silently roll down my face. This was the first time I had allowed myself to cry. I didn't even know why I was crying. Was I crying because my horrible secret was being let out? Was I crying because I knew this would hurt my parents? Was I crying because I was ashamed? Was I crying because now I was really scared what would happen to me at school? Was I crying because I was just so exhausted and overwhelmed? I guess I was crying about all these things.

Thankfully, Luke calmly told them that Shawn was sexually harassing me at school. Mom and Dad came and talked to me and said they were going to contact the principal and take care of this problem.

They were upset that I was being unwillingly touched, but they had no idea what the whole picture included!

January 12, 1994

Dad: Mom and I went to school to meet with Regina and the principal regarding what we thought was sexual harassment. You were also in Regina's office, but it was too difficult for you to talk about details of the incidents, so you stayed in her office during this "procedure." The school informed us that in accordance with their sexual harassment policy, Shawn was suspended for five days. It was also explained to us that he could appeal this disciplinary action … Shawn did appeal and the appeal hearing was set for January 19. On the day of Shawn's suspension, he initiated a verbal confrontation with Luke and threatened him and Rachel, calling Rachel a liar.

January 14, 1994

I'm feeling much better. I had a good talk last night with Gabe. He's really Luke's friend, but we're friends too.

January 16, 1994

I'm still tired from last night … or wait—it was Friday night. Gabe came over, and Luke, Gabe, and I watched the movie Cliffhanger. *Luke and I fell asleep, but Gabe stayed up later. I had a nightmare and woke up shaking. Gabe was there, and he helped me calm down. We started talking and didn't stop until 7:30 the next morning! At basketball practice the next day, I was so tired. I hate Saturday morning practices. I was so tired in church this morning, but I still taught Sunday school. I had breakfast and lunch today … the first time in a while. I've lost seven pounds. Today I'm just working on my history project and staying home to relax. I don't have bruises or dark circles under my eyes anymore … I won't have to hide it with cover-up. My life is beginning to get normal!*

January 18, 1994

I'm in a pretty good mood today. I got an A on my math test, a B on my Spanish test, and did well at basketball. Tomorrow at 10:00 a.m. is a hearing on whether or not this should be on Shawn's record. I'm scared. It could be either really good or really bad news. Mom thinks I like Gabe. I only talk to him; it's not as if I like him! He's more of a brother than anything else. I ate so much today. I ate a cup of granola, four Ritz crackers, corn, some meat, and two small red potatoes. I feel so bloated and that my stomach is getting big.

    I'm really scared about the hearing. What's going to happen? I'm really scared ... I don't know if I can do this ...

Wednesday, January 19, 1994

    Dad: When we came to the hearing, we had no idea what the agenda was to be ... We just came prepared to state the facts as we knew them at that time. Shawn had solicited signed statements from girls on the basketball team and Coach Carl that said, in effect, "Shawn is doing his job as scorekeeper and I have never seen him act inappropriately toward Rachel." He gave us the impression that he thought himself to be pretty clever.

    Before entering the room of the actual hearing, we were taken to Regina's office and were told that Rachel had been suicidal over the weekend and had confided this to her friend Travis. This came as quite a shock to us ... We agreed that the unwanted touching was bad and that no one should touch a person in an inappropriate place or manner, but suicide? That seemed an overreaction. It was with very heavy hearts and mixed emotions that we attended the hearing.

    At some point in the hearing (which was taped), it was mentioned that Rachel had been suicidal. Shawn reacted to the information by rolling his eyes. We felt very uncomfortable at the hearing because we felt we had revealed so much information about Rachel in Shawn's presence.

    The findings and decisions of the student disciplinary hearing included the stipulation that "Shawn should distance himself from Rachel and failure to do so can result in further disciplinary action." The principal also stated that Shawn would have an "in-school no-contact order" ... She also told us that the school security personnel would be informed of this and would help to enforce the decisions of the hearing. It was our main concern to guarantee safety for Rachel and that she could go to school and participate in basketball and be safe from Shawn and his threats. The principal assured us that with the no-contact order and with the advice given to Shawn and his mother that he take anger management classes, we could feel safe with our daughter at this school. In spite of her assurance, we still had uneasy feelings.

In the days following the hearing, Rachel became more depressed and withdrawn. We became concerned that she was overreacting to a situation that we thought had been settled. At the time, we were frustrated and troubled, having no idea what was really troubling Rachel.

Abigail: I remember being at a basketball game ... It must have been around the time you had the restraining order against Shawn. Mom and I were there to watch you play, and Shawn was sitting about three rows in front of us. Mom was extremely upset, and she pointed him out to me and said he's not supposed to be here and that he's bad. I just wanted to go down the bleachers by him and punch him.

A poem I wrote in January 1994:

My Deep Dark Life—Alone

I was alone and scared in that deep
Dark world of depression.
No one ventured near me,
For I always wore a sad expression.
No one reached out a hand
To help me out of my dark hole;
They thought I liked my life just fine,
Though I was just playing a role.
The people I used to call my friends,

They all turned against me.
Every day they teased and taunted;
No one knew how much I hurt.
They never saw the silent tears I shed.
At several times, I even thought of being dead
Because it seemed like no one cared.
But at the last moment,
I was pulled out of my dark world.
Someone showed me he cared.
Travis leant a hand to help me heal.
Now I know how precious life really is,
And I can't imagine
Ever trying to end my life again.

Chapter 11

Friday, January 21, 1994

S ince I had a restraining order against Shawn and he wasn't able to get near me, he wasn't able to be the trainer for basketball for the weeks' practices or for Friday's game. I was so relieved to get a little break from him! Actually, I had a little break from Coach Carl and Sebastian's harassment too. I thought things were getting better and maybe everything would just stop now that I began to tell.

It was Friday night, so we had another home basketball game. I played most of the JV game and really enjoyed myself. Since I had a week free from Shawn and Coach Carl harassing me, I was beginning to enjoy basketball. I was actually excited and pumped up to play varsity tonight.

During the varsity game, I was playing point guard and calling all the plays and playing quite well. Coach Carl was actually rather calm and didn't yell too often. I could feel myself let down my guard and relax. Shawn, who still had a restraining order and couldn't get within one hundred feet of me, had to sit in the bleachers and watch the game from a distance. I only looked and made sure he was near the top of the bleachers once, when the game began. When I saw he was so far up and not able to be near me, I didn't look again. However, during the game, he must have moved down closer to the basketball court. During one throw-in, I was at the sideline throwing the ball in and I could smell him. I glanced back and saw him just a few rows up. I saw him smirking at me and silently running his finger across his throat as a reminder to me to stay silent or else he would slice my throat. I instantly felt my body tense up, and my heart started racing. The ref's whistle jolted me back into the game, and I threw the ball in to my teammate. I continued playing and not thinking about Shawn.

But then he did it. Shawn finally got me to lose it. When the other team shot the ball and we were all scrambling for the rebound, Shawn whistled loudly. I turned and looked at him. He was on the lowest row of bleachers and smiling at me. I instantly lost it. I forgot where I was; all I could see were flashbacks of me being repeatedly raped by him. I couldn't breathe. I couldn't stop shaking. I completely lost it. I wasn't present anymore; I was back to that dreadful night of December 13. I couldn't stop shaking, and I somehow ended up in the little room adjacent to the gym. I remember sitting in a chair beside a little wooden table and having Travis in there with me. I could hear him talking to me, but I couldn't distinguish any actual words. I couldn't erase those awful memories. I felt as if I were back in the fine arts building and being raped all over again. I found out later that the principal was called and she called my parents. My dad came and sat with me in that little room. Dad and Travis were scared since I wasn't talking—only crying and mumbling repeatedly, "I need to end this!" According to my dad and Travis, my lips were white, my eyes were rolled back, and I was shaking uncontrollably. This was the first time I allowed myself to actually remember what happened to me that horrid night. I always knew that something happened and that I was scared and feeling sick whenever I saw them, but I never really allowed myself to go there and remember what happened. Now that I knew, I was terrified.

I finally calmed down, and my dad took me to Denny's so we could talk. We were the only customers in the restaurant, and we sat down in a booth in the far corner, away from any other tables. Dad had coffee, and I had clam chowder. I had never had clam chowder, but it sounded good to have something nice and hot to warm my ice-cold body from fear. We sat there in silence for a little while, me eating my chowder and Dad slowly drinking his coffee and watching me with tender, scared, concerned brown eyes.

Dad cleared his throat and began talking. I wanted to scream at him to just stop talking and to leave me alone. But I didn't. Instead, I just sat there quietly, lost in my own memories of misery, not hearing anything he was saying. I noticed that he stopped talking, and I looked at him. He looked so concerned and so full of fatherly love that my eyes teared up, my lips quivered, and I opened my mouth to talk ... but I had no words. *What should I say to my dad? How do I even begin? I know he wants to help me, but I can't let him know how awful this is.* I don't remember much of what we said to each other that night. All I know is that I didn't tell him much of anything, yet he felt we made great progress that night. His famous saying that night was, "Well, Rachel ... we're at the top of the mountain now. It's all downhill from here." To this day, we joke about that comment! We certainly were at the top of the mountain, and we had no idea of the terrifying, death-defying roller coaster ride ahead of us!

Dad: I was sitting across from you along the window side of the restaurant across from the counter; my back was toward the front entrance. I don't remember what we ate, but all I could think was that as your dad, I was expected to have something very profound to say, but was scared to think I might say or do the wrong thing. I was way, way out of my comfort zone and said umpteen silent prayers for the right words to say. Maybe that's where I came up with the "top of the mountain" saying. I desperately tried to tell you that we loved you and that we'd always be there for you, but I was feeling as if I failed to get that message across to you. It seemed that you had a difficult time looking at me. I really don't remember much more than this ... just that I was relieved when it was time to go home. Again, still very concerned and worried about what we thought ... at that time ... that it was an overreaction regarding what we thought was a settled issue and the fact that you had been spending what we felt to be an inordinate amount of time in Regina's office, we scheduled an appointment with a child psychologist to discuss our concerns with him. The appointment was scheduled for February 2.

Mom: I remember talking to Travis and saying that it's as if Rachel has many different personalities. She can be so studious yet be so silly. She can be so easygoing but then be serious and stubborn. She has so many wonderful traits, but I just can't put my finger on it—something is going on. I feel I could drop dead and she'd just walk over my dead body. She has such a wild look, as if she has wolf eyes. She's so kind yet so distant and cold.

Chapter 12

Friday, January 28, 1994

We had an away game, and Mom dropped me off several minutes before we were expected at the game for warm-ups while she ran some errands. While I was waiting for the rest of the JV team to show up, I decided to just start stretching. I went behind the scorekeeping table and used the first row of bleachers for stretching. The next thing I knew, I heard Shawn. He came over to me and smirked, "You better watch out tonight! You might get slapped around or worse." He lifted his white hooded sweatshirt from his waist, exposing the butt of his gun in his pants waistband. Travis and Gabe were sitting several rows behind Shawn and heard his comment. They asked if I was okay. I was so scared and nervous. *What is he going to do to me now? He wouldn't dare shoot me in front of people, would he? He can't be that crazy! I just want to go home! I can't tell anyone!* By the time the game started, Mom was back. I played the JV game but then talked to Mom and said I wanted to go home, telling her I had a bad headache. Mom talked to Coach Carl and told him I was going home and not playing varsity that night.

Dad: Late in the evening, Rachel was on the phone with Travis and began to open up to him about Shawn being at the game on Friday night and how he scared her. Later that night, she told us that Shawn had threatened her. She was hesitant to tell us since Mom and I had a two-day trip planned for a pastors' conference out of state. She was worried that if she told us about the threats, we would cancel our trip. The next morning, we called the principal and told her about Shawn threatening Rachel.

Saturday, January 29, 1994

We usually didn't have practice on Saturdays, but since we'd played so poorly the night before, Coach Carl said there would be practice just for the guards. I like to be punctual, and I was scared of receiving Coach Carl's wrath for being late, so I made sure Mom would get me to school on time for the 7:00 a.m. practice.

When we got to the school, we noticed that the parking lot was still chained closed and we didn't see any other cars parked near the school. Mom kept asking if I was sure I had practice that morning. She was there and heard Coach Carl say we had practice, so I was irritated with her for asking me. I argued with her and pleaded with her to just drop me off since the other girls would be coming soon. Mom didn't like the idea of dropping me off when it was obvious that no one else was around, so we argued back and forth. I was getting worried that Coach Carl was in the gym and that I would get punished for keeping him waiting. I grew frantic and more insistent about getting dropped off. I jumped out of the car before Mom could answer me, and I waved good-bye to her. As I jogged to the gym door, Mom left and went home.

I tried to open the door, but it was locked. I looked in the back parking lot and saw that it was empty. Not a single car in either parking lot. I went to the stairs that lead to the downstairs gym and to the locker room. Locked. *Now what should I do? Where is everybody? He said we had practice today, didn't he?* I started to doubt that there was practice, and I started wishing that I had listened to my mom. I should have had her wait with me. *I shouldn't have yelled at her. She wasn't in a hurry … Why didn't I have her wait? Where is everybody? Coach Carl said there was practice for the guards, didn't he? I hope I don't get in trouble for being late. I can't help it that the doors are locked. Is anyone in the gym? Is anyone coming this morning? What should I do? Should I stay and wait to see if someone comes … or should I walk home? Ahhh … I'm starting to get cold out here!*

As I was walking around, trying all the doors and trying to figure out what to do, I heard a car door slam shut. *Oh, good! Someone else has come for practice!* I looked and saw my homeroom teacher's old van parked in the driveway up against the chain that blocked the parking lot entrance. Coach Carl, Shawn, Sebastian, and my homeroom teacher were walking toward me. *Oh no! Hurry up and hide! Help! Where should I go?* Feeling scared, I ran back to the stairwell that goes down to the lower gym. I quickly ran down the stairs and tried to hide from them. I tried not to breathe since I was sure they could hear my heart pounding. I hoped to God that they didn't see me. *Please don't see me! Please go and leave me alone! Please don't hurt me!*

I sat in the corner of the stairwell, shivering in the cold, straining to hear them so I would know where they were, and I tried to formulate a plan to escape. My heart kept pounding away, and I couldn't stop shaking. I was sure they would hear me and capture me. I kept thinking that if I didn't see them, they couldn't see me.

Then I heard Shawn laugh. I guess I was wrong; they did see me. I looked up and saw "the gang" looking down at me. Shawn sneered at me and said that this would be easier than he thought. They came down the steps and pushed me up against the cold cement wall. *What do I do? There's no place to run or hide! Help!* They pretended to slap me, and I flinched. They proceeded to hit me in the face, shoulder, chest, and stomach whenever I flinched. I never knew when they would actually hit me or not, so it was difficult not to flinch. It took me awhile, but I eventually learned that if I just stood there and didn't flinch, they would leave me alone. Shawn kept yelling at me, "That's right. Lay there and enjoy it!" Shawn kissed me and then spit in my face. Sebastian pushed me up against the wall again and began pulling on my warm-up pants. Shawn and Coach Carl held me against the cold cement wall while Sebastian tried to untie my drawstring holding my pants. They only had my upper body pinned against the wall, so I used my legs to fight back. *Get away from me! Leave me alone!* I kept kicking at them, so Sebastian had a difficult time getting close enough to untie the drawstring. I didn't even realize at first that while I was fighting them, I was being punched and slammed into the wall. They were yelling and swearing at me to shut up and that they would have no choice but to kill me if I kept screaming and fighting. After my head was slammed especially hard against the wall, I must have blacked out and stopped fighting. All went silent. Everything was darkness. I could feel my body falling, but I couldn't stop it.

As I sat there hunched over with my head pounding and feeling it was going to explode, I was given another rude awakening. A hard object hit me on the side of my head. I thought all my teeth were going to fall out and that my jaw was broken. My eyes focused, and I saw the barrel of a gun held against my forehead. It was the scariest dull black gun I had ever seen. As I stared at the gun, I saw that it was held by my homeroom teacher and that Sebastian was standing behind him. I was so terrified of that gun that I began to shake uncontrollably with terror. *These guys are insane! They're seriously going to kill me! I'm going to die in this stairwell! Oh, God, help me!*

I have never been so terrified in all my life. To be more accurate, the word *terrified* doesn't even come close to describing my fear. It was death defying knowing that my life was in their hands … their evil-minded hands. My homeroom teacher was calm and kept telling me, "That's right. Calm down. Relax and stop fighting. Just listen and do what we say." I felt as if his calm voice hypnotized me, and I calmed down. I returned to breathing normally, and I stopped shaking. I was let go, and I just sat there in the corner trapped. He calmly told me, "The quicker you learn to be quiet and obedient, the easier it will be for you. Otherwise, you'll have to take a visit in my van." He asked if I understood, and I nodded my head.

A few days earlier, I began questioning Coach Carl. He responded by taking me for a ride in my homeroom teacher's van, and it terrified me. He had an old black work van. The inside of the van was lined with yellowish-orange-and-white marbled-looking rubbery material that he said made the van soundproof. Metal bars bolted to the floor separated the back from the front. On the other side of the metal bars was more of that soundproofing material, so I couldn't see outside. On the floor of the van was a thin mattress with a crinkly blue tarp. I was thrown onto the tarp-covered mattress, and my wrists were handcuffed to the bars. I don't remember everything that happened in this van, but I do remember him saying, "If you need a second reminder, you won't return." I just remember being terrified of this van and not wanting to ever go for a second ride.

I was told to untie my pants. I did. Sebastian yanked off my pants and swore at me. I guess he wasn't expecting me to be wearing so many layers of clothes. I wanted to kick him so bad, but I kept glancing at my homeroom teacher holding the gun. He saw me looking at him, so he put the gun to his lips and said, "Shh." I don't know what made me tremble more: being half-naked outside in the middle of winter or fear of being shot, raped, and dying. *What is wrong with you jerks? How can you be so evil? What did I ever do to you? I'm so sorry!*

Sebastian unzipped my jacket and then took it off. He kept swearing at me as he undressed me. Coach Carl told him to leave me alone. I was left in the corner completely naked while they huddled together and talked quietly while looking in a black duffel bag. *Okay ... now what am I supposed to do? Are you finished with me? What should I do? Do I just stay here or should I run for it?*

I thought they were finished terrorizing me since they had left me alone and were just talking to themselves and going in and out of the gym door. I didn't know if I was supposed to just stand there and freeze or if I was allowed to get dressed and run home. I quietly and carefully began to pull my jacket closer to me. I thought that if I could grab it, I could at least stay warmer. I even thought that I could maybe run past them and up the steps. I finally had my jacket in my hand, unnoticed by everyone! I almost got giddy with excitement that my plan was working, and I could even imagine myself running to freedom. I counted to three in my head, and then I bolted for the steps.

I made up my mind that I wouldn't stop for anything. *Let them shoot and kill me—a lot easier than suicide. At least I'd die trying!* I got up a few steps, and then I was pulled down. My body hit every ice-covered cement step. I was freezing and hurting and terrified, but I wouldn't stop. I had had enough of this. I was thrown down to the ground, but I instantly got back up and ran toward the steps again. I almost got to the top of the steps, but then I was grabbed around the ankles and pulled back down. Looking back, I'm sure it was part of their torture: let me think that I was close to freedom and then at the last minute pull me down the steps and back into their grasp. It was like a cat playing with a mouse ... except unrelenting monsters were playing with me.

I was slammed into the cement wall, and Coach Carl held the gun to my forehead. He was swearing and yelling at me for not learning my lesson. He was about to pistol-whip me, but my homeroom teacher grabbed his arm. He snatched the gun and calmly told me to be a good girl, lie down, and be obedient. He saw me lying there shaking, and he covered me up with my jacket. He calmly squatted next to me and explained that I needed to cooperate in order to help my friend Amanda. He then played a tape recording of Amanda being raped. He explained that she had a large debt and that I could help her if I cooperated for my special sessions.

What is this huge debt they keep threatening me with? What did we do wrong?

"It's all very easy," he kept telling me. Just as Shawn was about to lie down on top of me, I pulled up my leg and kneed him in the groin. He rolled to the side, held himself, and swore at me. It felt so good to hurt him and to stop him from hurting me! *Yes! Get off me, you jerk! Leave me alone!*

That satisfaction was short-lived, for I was quickly kicked and had the gun pointed at me. I was paralyzed with fear. Coach Carl held the gun, threatening me that he had his fingers on the trigger and that if I moved, he would shoot me. I tried so hard to control my breathing and to be as still as possible as he traced my body with the gun. I hated myself for being so terrified. I hated myself for not being able to get away from them. I hated myself for being so stupid and always finding myself in such predicaments. *Why do I have to be so stupid? Come on, Rachel ... Don't give him the satisfaction of seeing you scared! Be tough!*

With Coach Carl's orders, Shawn raped me while Coach Carl held the gun in my mouth. *Oh, God, please help me! Get them to stop! Please help me stay still! I don't want to die! I don't want to die like this! Please help me!* I was so scared. I was even scared to breathe since I didn't want to make even the slightest movement. All I could focus on was lying there as still as possible and trying not to breathe.

Coach Carl laughed. "Looks like we found what works for her!"

I was so mad at myself for being broken and for just lying there not fighting. *Why didn't I fight back more? Why didn't I try kicking him again? Why do I keep doing everything they say? What's wrong with me? I'm so dumb!*

Shawn got dressed, and I was told to say my number. I was so worn out, freezing, hurting, scared, and numb from fear, but I did as I was told and said one-eight-nine-eight-six-eight. They were over by the black bag working with the video recorder. *Lovely … just lovely. They just recorded my being raped. Now they have more blackmail against me and I'll have a larger debt to have to pay off! How am I ever supposed to pay it off? Who are they going to show the video and pictures to? Will my parents see it? What would they say? Would they kick me out of the family? Will they believe me that I didn't want to do this? This is never going to end … I need to do something!*

I saw them go into the lower gym, leaving only Shawn in the stairwell with me. I thought this would be my last chance, so I darted for the steps. I almost got to the top when I heard Shawn yelling, "Get the Glock! Get the Glock! I'm going to kill her!" I never looked back; I just kept running for the trees by the swimming pool building. *Why does there have to be ice and snow? It hardly ever snows here!* I focused on not slipping on the ice and continued to run away from those monsters.

"Stop or I'll shoot!" yelled Shawn.

I was almost to the trees, and I glanced back and saw Shawn holding the gun pointed at me, standing in the parking lot. I turned around and kept running for the trees. *Come on—run faster! Hurry! Is he really going to shoot me? Oh, God, help me get to the trees!* I was just entering the trees when I heard a couple of loud pops and instantly felt a hot streak across my right side of my head just above my ear. I stumbled into the trees and then fell down. I grabbed my head and felt a sticky sore area. I looked at my fingers and saw pink-tinted fluid. *He just shot at me! The bullet must have skimmed my head. I can't believe he just shot at me! Oh my! I was just shot at! These guys are insane!* I was so numb—not sure if it was from the cold or fear. I crouched behind some trees watching them. My homeroom teacher hit Shawn across the face, and it looked as if they were all arguing. They all climbed into the old black van. I watched them drive off, not knowing what to think or do. I was freezing, but I was too scared to move from the protection of the trees. *What should I do? Run and get my clothes? What if they come back? What if someone sees me? How long do I hide here? Are they going to finish me off tomorrow? What else will they do to me? Did this really happen? Why do I keep walking into their traps? How can I be so stupid?*

After a few minutes of waiting and making sure they didn't come back, I snuck back to the stairwell and quickly got dressed. *Now what do I do?* I had no idea what time it was or how soon Mom would be back to pick me up. I kept telling myself I needed to think and make a plan. I felt safer in the cover of the trees, so I quickly went back. I thought of just lying down in the bushes and willing myself to die. I couldn't keep living like this. I felt as if it would never end. I didn't foresee any ending except them killing me. As I burrowed deeper into the bushes, I began to feel a certain calmness come over my body. I was able to think clearly and realized I couldn't stay hiding here forever. I made a plan to calmly walk to the swimming pool building and call Mom to pick me up.

I got to the swimming pool building and walked into the lobby. I went to the pay phone to call my mom, but once again, I didn't have any money. I went to the counter and asked the guy if I could borrow the phone. The guy behind the counter handed it to me. I held the phone in my hand and was about to dial the number for home, but I just stood there listening to the buzz of the dial tone as though I were frozen. I couldn't remember my own phone number! I don't know how long I stood there, but I finally realized that the guy was asking me if I was okay. I must have dropped the phone, for it was dangling on the cord over the counter. I never answered the guy, but as if I were walking in a cloud, I left the pool and went to the Langleys' house.

When I reached their home, I banged on the door until they opened it. I didn't even wait to be asked in; I just barged my way in and frantically said that I needed my mom *now*. They asked if I was okay and called my mom. By this time, I had pushed all that had happened into the very far corner of my conscious memory. I didn't allow myself to think about what had happened. All I remembered was that I was angry at my mom for dropping me off and not waiting until someone else had come for practice. I was angry that there wasn't practice and that no one else came. I just knew that I was angry. (We later found out that Coach Carl had called the other players and cancelled the practice).

Monday, January 31, 1994

As I was getting ready for school, Mom came into my room and told me that she was watching the news and that my homeroom teacher was shot and killed Sunday night. She was shocked and couldn't believe it. Many people, including my mom, thought that he was a great director of student affairs and a great role model for troubled teens.

I didn't know what to think or feel. I was confused since so many people were sad about his dying. I couldn't stand him, and I feared him. No, he didn't actually touch me or rape me, but I felt that he was the ringleader and that he orchestrated all the attacks on me. I had even thought that in order to stop all the abuse, I would have to do something to him. I was relieved that he was dead and that I wouldn't have to do anything to him myself.

When I got to school, everybody was talking about the shooting that took place Sunday evening. I'm not sure why, but hearing about his death gave me courage to tell someone that I was raped. I still didn't remember him or Coach Carl being involved in the rapes. I just remembered Shawn and Sebastian raping me. It was too much for my brain to handle, so I had broken memories of what had happened to me.

We later found out that my homeroom teacher was shot and killed by a former student who was abused by him. The former student had shot him because he didn't know how else to end the abuse that had occurred over many years. When the police went to my homeroom teacher's house after the shooting, they discovered a house full of boxes with pictures and notebooks with names and number sequences next to the names. One police officer told the newspaper that what they saw in the house was creepy and sickening. The house was taped off, but during the night, it was broken into and completely emptied and cleaned out.

That night, I called Travis and talked to him for a long time. I began to open up to him about Shawn. I thought that if I just talked about Shawn, it would be more believable and I could test Travis to see if he was trustworthy. I didn't actually say that I was raped, but I alluded to that fact.

Unknown to me, early that morning while I was at school, Mom wrote a letter to the school principal:

Dear Ms. Caters:

> *I feel we have been very patient in dealing with "due process" and the way the situation is being handled in regards to our daughter's safety at the high school.*
>
> *I believe our daughter's safety at this school is in jeopardy because of Shawn. None of us were surprised that he had broken his restraining order and verbally threatened Rachel at the basketball game on Friday. We were all relieved that it was only a verbal threat … this time. But what about the next time? I don't want to just sit back waiting for the next time he breaks his restraining order.*
>
> *I can only imagine what it must be like to be a fifteen-year-old freshman and to go to school always in fear of another student who has already treated you in an inappropriate, disrespecting, controlling way and to be feeling like a sitting duck just waiting for another one of his outbursts of out-of-control anger to erupt.*
>
> *Shawn is still the one in control of the whole situation. We are all feeling victimized just waiting for the next verbal or physical assault. And you know, as well as I, that there will be one because Shawn has not seen his problem in how his actions are affecting another student.*
>
> *I can only imagine how this is affecting Rachel, because as her parents, we are trying in a calm way to be reassuring and rational that "due process" is working and that everything is going to be okay. But it isn't okay.*

We should be able to drop her off at her basketball game and know that she is in a safe place. But then we find out that Shawn had already been there at least thirty minutes prior to the start of the game and had made a threatening comment. His presence at the game is intimidating and totally affects us all. This is her school, her team, yet Shawn has control over all this.

With Shawn's lack of respect for Rachel and from his prior school history, lack of respect for teachers and authority, it greatly concerns me that our daughter is just a sitting duck waiting for someone who is in need of "anger management and control" to just lose it one more time.

I cannot just sit patiently waiting for the next time Shawn breaks his restraining order. It is so hard sending your child off to school each day when you know there is someone at school who is threatening and is capable of doing harm. At the hearing, I expressed my main concern: that I want our daughter to be able to go to school in a safe environment. I have not seen anything happening over the past weeks that convinces me that that is the case.

In my estimation of the situation, I don't see any changes in Shawn that convince me that he is sorry for what he has done. He has not seen his part in how his actions have had an effect on a fellow classmate.

I firmly believe that Shawn's presence at this school is threatening to a fellow student and that because of his verbal threats, a student is in danger. He does not belong at this school.

Chapter 13

Tuesday, February 1, 1994

When I got to school the next morning, Travis found me right away and we talked. He told me that what I told him the night before was serious and that I needed to report it to Regina, the school nurse. I kept telling him that I was okay and that I was probably overreacting. I said it wasn't a big deal and that he just needed to forget what I told him. Throughout the day, I tried to avoid him so that I didn't have to talk about it again, and I hoped that he would just forget what I told him. *Why did I have to open my big mouth? Now what's going to happen? I don't want this to mess up my relationship I have with Travis … I really like him, and I don't want him to get hurt. What if Shawn and Coach Carl find out that I told Travis?*

I was able to dodge Travis until I had Spanish with him. Before class started, Travis talked to me outside the classroom and tried to drag me into the nurse's office. I shrugged him off and went into class. Instead of going to class, Travis went to Regina's office. A few minutes after class started, a student "runner," a student who would run notes from the office to the classrooms and help out in the office, came and gave Senora Sanchez a note. She came over to my desk and said that Regina requested to see me in her office. I was told to leave and go to her office. I walked to her office with dread and stubbornness to be tough and not say anything. *Don't say anything, Rachel! You need to keep Abigail safe! It'll be all your fault if she gets hurt. Be strong!*

Travis met me in the hall outside her office door. He gave me a hug, apologized for betraying my trust, and said that I would be okay. He had tears in his crystal-blue eyes as he pleaded with me to tell her everything and that I would feel so much better afterward.

We entered Regina's office together. I was trembling with fear. Travis and I sat down across from Regina's desk. Regina wasn't in her office since she was finishing taking care of a sick student. As we sat alone waiting, Travis opened his book bag and took out two brown stuffed animals. He told me these were early Valentine's Day presents and that they were "love puppies." They were soft and cute magnetic puppies, and when they were pulled apart, they would go back to each other. I thought that was so kind of him and appreciated his thoughtfulness.

I sat there in the orange fabric-covered chair holding the puppies, still numb with fear. *I can't say anything! What am I going to do? What if they find out that I told? Now what's going to happen?* When Regina walked in, Travis left. *No, please don't leave me! I feel safe when I'm with you! Why did you have to tell Regina? I can't believe that you told her! Please don't leave me!*

I did *not* want to talk to Regina! I was so scared to tell her what happened. I still didn't remember all that had happened to me. I was terrified that Shawn would find out that I told. *What do I even tell her? It doesn't even make sense to me! I just remember short moments of terror ... I don't even remember where it happened or everybody who was there! It's too painful to think about. It's not going to make any sense. Maybe it's just a bad dream or it didn't really happen to me. How could this have happened? Am I going crazy?*

I sat there and absentmindedly pulled out the fur on the puppies. I didn't say anything for the longest time; I just had a blank stare as I pulled out the fur. I didn't even realize what I was doing ... I just kept having flashbacks of being raped by Shawn. I didn't even realize that Regina came into her office and that I started talking to Regina. But then I saw that she was understanding. She believed me, and she wasn't judging me. I remember sitting there shaking like a leaf and talking in short quiet phrases while watching the brown puppy fur pile up into a mound on the floor. I knew I was talking to Regina, but what I was saying and even what I was doing didn't sink into my conscience brain.

I was so numb. I was in such shock, and the more I talked to her, the more memories came flooding back. My flashbacks would be a little of one attack and then suddenly be memories of another attack, with images and intense body memories swarming my brain and body. While in her office, I was reliving every single horrible attack. Those flashbacks were more than just memories … It was living through the pain all over again. The sights, smells, tastes, sounds, and touches of those horrendous events come flooding back. I wasn't just remembering the rapes; I was experiencing them, reliving every single hit in the face, hearing the degrading comments, feeling the extreme pain—both physical and emotional pain. It was confusing for me, and I'm sure it was confusing for Regina, trying to piece everything together and make sense of it all. She hugged me and told me how brave I was, saying that it wasn't my fault and that I did the right thing by telling her.

She had me sit and wait in the empty sick room. I sat on the cot closest to the door and just stared at the closed door. *What's going to happen now? How do I make this stop? I'm so scared. I don't know what to do. I need help, but I don't want my sister to get hurt!* There was a knock on the door, and in walked two policemen. I was shocked and scared since I was expecting my parents, not police officers! *Ahhh! Get away from me! Leave me alone! Help!* The two police officers came into the sick room, closed the door, and then stood by the door. Looking at them, I was terrified. They looked so tall standing there in their uniforms with their guns at their hips, and I was sitting on a cot in a small sick room with the door closed and blocked by their bodies. I felt trapped, and I didn't trust them. *As if I can trust you! You're probably just as dirty as Detective Clark! I'll never trust police! Get away from me!* They asked me so many embarrassing questions and had me tell them what had happened to me. I told them I was raped by Shawn in the fine arts building on December 13. I have no idea what they wrote down in their notepads, but they were scribbling away while asking me questions. I was so relieved when I heard a knock on the door and they stopped asking questions.

Mom: That afternoon, I was watching the news reports about Rachel's homeroom teacher being shot. I was spellbound by the reports since that was Rachel's teacher. We lived in a rough neighborhood, but it wasn't as if we had daily shootings. I had a horrible cold, and I never get sick, so I was enjoying being able to just sort of veg out on the couch and watch the news. Then I got the phone call ... I don't remember if it was Regina or the principal who called, but the caller just said, "Rachel needs you here at school. It's really important that you get here now." They didn't say that you were raped, but I had the sinking feeling that it was more involved than just the sexual harassment. I felt as if I already knew you were raped but that I just needed to have it confirmed ... needed to be told ... needed to hear those horrible words. I remember getting in the car with Dad and telling him, "I bet Rachel was raped and that she's pregnant. She hasn't had her period for two months." I began to shake uncontrollably as we drove to school. Once we got to school and went to the office, I saw Travis and police officers. Being a mom, my reaction was very different from Dad's. My first reaction was, "I just want to see Rachel. I need to be by Rachel." I didn't even think about Shawn or what he did. I was just so focused on being with you.

The police officers opened the door, and I saw my parents enter the main office as Regina stood at the door of the sick room. My mom ran into the room crying, and my dad was so angry and yelling that he wanted to know what was going on and wanted to know where I was. It felt as if it were in slow motion as I watched every emotion on my parents' faces. At first, I saw anger, and then it went from panic to grief to shock. It's hard to explain how all those emotions were shown in such a brief moment, but the memory of seeing my parents' reaction will haunt me until the day I die. Mom quickly ran to me. She held me and sobbed. I had never seen Mom cry so hard before. Dad was furious and was walking around yelling that he wanted to see Shawn and saying that he was going to kill him. He came into the sick room by Mom and me and gave me a hug. He was about to sit down next to Mom and me on the cot, but then he got up and went over to the brick wall and began punching it. The officer stopped him, and Dad tried to get out of the room and go after Shawn. The officer blocked the doorway, and Dad just stood there shaking and crying. I felt so horrible for causing my parents so much pain and heartache. Watching them hurt so much was almost worse than being raped and tortured. While I was talking to my parents, Shawn was hauled away in handcuffs. He went to juvenile detention.

Dad: I really don't remember when I first heard that you were raped ... It must have been soon after, when I was sitting in an office at the high school with the principal behind the desk, me in front of the desk, and a cop between me and the door to the next room where Shawn was. I remember saying to the cop, "It's a good thing you're standing where you are or I'd be in the next room taking Shawn apart!" His response was, "That's why I'm standing where I am." I kept thinking, How does a father deal with the idea that his daughter has been violated? *In the index of the "father manual," there was no alphabetical listing or entry for this! Anger, rage, and inadequacy in providing you defense, hatred, and so forth ... Besides the anger I felt in finding out that you'd been raped were all the classic things that a person goes through in processing "bad news" ... including denial. Could this really be true? Did it really happen? Well, it must be true. Why else would the cops be there? Why else would the principal have called us into her office? As a dad, I felt that I had somehow let you down by not protecting you ... I was feeling very frustrated! I remember sitting there not only as a dad but also as a pastor and wondering how I should be acting and thinking ... The whole day was all so confusing! Lots of broken pieces ... How would the pieces ever be put back together again?*

Mom: I remember thinking that I needed to arrange for someone to pick up Abigail and Ben from school. I couldn't stop shaking, and as I was handed a phone book to call someone, I couldn't think. I was so helpless. This horrible thing happened to you, and now I couldn't even take care of my kids. I couldn't even remember how to use a phone book. I just flipped through the pages, not even being able to think about whom to call.

All I remember about the car ride home is that Mom kept asking, "How could this happen?" She was asking no one in particular the same questions repeatedly the entire time, and Dad kept talking about getting a gun and killing Shawn. I quietly sat in the back seat, thankfully being ignored.

Mom: When we got home and I saw Abigail and Ben, I realized that we still needed to eat and that I needed to provide for my kids. We hardly ever ate out, but we got food from Burger King. It's like the movie Sleeping Beauty *... when time froze when she touched the spinning wheel. That's how I felt. Time froze. We were frozen in the darkest, most horrible, unimaginable moment.*

Dad: When we got home, two male detectives came to the house and parked their unmarked black van in the church parking lot ... Only later did I learn that a black van was part of your memories. They interviewed you at the house, downstairs at the big table in my office. Mom and I were home, but we weren't allowed to listen in. It required a lot of trust on our part to let them talk to you alone ... You were quite shaken up when they finally left.

Chapter 14

Days following telling my parents

The next day, I was interviewed by a new detective whom I liked a lot more than the first two detectives. Detective Gouch was a no-nonsense tough-looking tall woman, but she listened to me and believed me. She would become the detective assigned to our case, and I had several conversations with her.

February 2, 1994

Dad: We met with the psychologist and gave him an overview of what we knew at the time. Our original purpose for meeting with a counselor had changed, and he recommended another counselor who specializes in this area. We made an appointment with Dr. McConnell for February 8.

Mom's journal dated February 2, 1994:

I wish I could pray or just cry, but I can't. If I cry, I'll never want to stop. I try to pray, but my mind is so full of too many thoughts to separate anything to make any sense. However, I feel the presence of God. No pit is so deep that God can't be in it with you. Those words from the movie Hiding Place *have given me comfort and strength, and they will be our whole family's motto.*

I have gut feelings, and they are always right. I believe that Rachel is pregnant. My first thought without thinking is to end the pregnancy. It would be a quick fix to a big, serious problem. But what is the difference between ending the life or committing suicide as a quick fix to end life's problems? It is on the same parallel. Only God gives life and takes it away. As people, we can't be the ones to be in that ultimate control. Only God knows what He has planned. We don't always understand how and why … It is so hard to understand how God works. How could He use such a violent act to bring life into the world? I always thought that if I would be raped, I wouldn't continue with the pregnancy, but I see now that death of a baby is not the answer. Will the sacrifice of a baby change what has happened? No—it will only compound the pain. It will only make the next seven months of rehabilitation be less obvious to people from the outside. But what about you, my dear Rachel—does that seem like an answer? Then sometimes I'm overwhelmed with such grief that I think no children should ever be born to this awful world. I look at Abigail and Ben with not delight and excitement with all the possibilities that lie out there in the world for them … but rather with horror and dread knowing what is really out there.

I'm so exhausted. My body feels like an empty shell … Maybe if I stay in this state of exhaustion, I will never feel the intensity of the real pain. Oh, how I envy Ray—he was able to feel real hate and anger, and he cried like a baby. Do I love less because I don't feel? I'm numb. I have to be strong. Rachel needs me more now than ever. When a child is sick and you are up all night, you don't put your needs in front. You just concentrate on taking care of that child.

It's weird. The house seems so still, so dead. The walls that breathed life seem to be in hibernation, like in Sleeping Beauty, when the castle was asleep for one hundred years. Time has stopped. And time will get turned back on, and there will be laughter and songs and parties—but right now it has stopped.

I need to record in this journal about Rachel—my source of strength. She is truly amazing, and when she sets all her wonderful qualities into gear, she will be dynamite. She has a steadfast strength in her that runs so deep. So much young, undeveloped maturity. And then she has the playfulness of a young girl. Just seeing her on the phone the other night, being so happy and being able to enjoy life as a teen, was so refreshing.

I had felt there was a distance between Rachel and me. I couldn't put my finger on it. Those gut feelings really are real—listen to them!

Am I nuts or is it okay to write my feelings down? I cry—I haven't really cried yet for Rachel. I cry. Shawn has taken the life, the life, out of our castle, our home, and it seems so dead. Yet I think of Ben. He wanted to wake up early to see if the groundhog could see his shadow today. How can the castle all be sleeping and then there is this innocent little boy who can't wait till morning? Oh, the joys of being a child. Childlike faith ... How can we ever have childlike faith when we know how bitter and ugly the world really is? I hate this world and all the violence ... How can the devil have such control?

I need to write or I feel like my thoughts will take over my mind. I must empty my head of my feelings so I can deal with the facts and hard times of the new day.

February 4, 1994

Mom's journal: God started out yesterday with a miracle. Rachel got her period! Praise the Lord! What rejoicing and praising God. A good day today. We went to the prosecuting attorney, and Rachel was interviewed for one and a half hours. She did really well. The attorney said Rachel even smiled a little. When they got to the day of the rape, Rachel started to tremble. Great people. We feel good. Rachel said it was the worst day, but the best day being able to give her problem to someone else. She has such profound wisdom in the little she does say. We almost thought we were going to go to the hearing when Shawn made his first appearance. We wanted to tell the judge what a threat it would be to have Shawn released. He is so violent. He already had his first hearing yesterday—relief. I don't know if Ray could have been in the same room with Shawn. Rachel was seen by an OB-GYN and had a pelvic exam. She had blood work done to test for STDs and was given a shot for prevention of gonorrhea and a prescription for prevention of other sexually transmitted diseases ... Testing for HIV will be in several months. This exam was very difficult for Rachel. Oh, the pain—my heart is being pulled out of me again ...

I'm glad I came to peace with myself about the thought of Rachel being pregnant. I never knew if I really would be pro-life in that situation. It was strengthening to me to know that. Rachel said she and Travis talked about it. They both agreed that abortion is wrong. Rachel said it would have been hard to give away a baby she had, but she knew she would never love it. Such big thoughts for a young person.

I talked to Mom today for the first time. I feel upset and agitated when she asks some questions, but considering everything, she took it okay. God truly carried us this day.

This gynecological exam was more than difficult for me—it was traumatizing! I remember lying on the exam table and just trembling and having flashback after flashback flood my mind. In my mind, I was being raped all over again. This was not a good first gynecological exam experience! Besides the fear from the constant flashbacks, the shame of having to be tested for HIV and STDs, and the fear of possibly having an STD, I was quite overwhelmed with this doctor's visit. *How am I supposed to explain my period? Did I really get my period or is it still the aftereffects of what the "Doctor" did? How can I tell Coach Carl and the "Doctor" that I haven't had my period for two months? Sure, they knew already since Coach Carl keeps record of all the girls' menstruating cycles, but how could I just stand there as they said they'd fix that problem? Was I really pregnant? Did they really perform an abortion like they said? Or did they just do that to scare me and fill me with so much shame? I don't believe in abortion, but how could I watch my belly grow and know that I was carrying Shawn's baby? He's such a monster. I don't want any part of him in my body! I'm still sore from the "Doctor's" procedure, and I'm still bleeding ... Maybe I wasn't really pregnant and they just hurt me and scared me! I feel so horrible about this ... How can I go to church knowing there's a chance I was pregnant and that I didn't do anything when they said they'd take care of the problem? How will I ever forgive myself? At least my parents can stop worrying ...*

(When I had an OB-GYN appointment years later, the doctor told me that I would have a difficult time getting pregnant since I had so much scar tissue damage. He was very upset when examining me since, according to him, "It looks like someone took a cheese grater to you." I had to have surgery to repair some damage … It was never confirmed if I was pregnant or not. I just had the emotional and physical scars as proof of what they did to me.)

Mom's journal:

It's 10:00 p.m. Rachel started to feel real down and talked to Travis. I thanked him. He was an angel. He was her lifesaver. God used Travis; most kids/people wouldn't have seen Rachel through this turmoil … I didn't. She frustrated me. I wouldn't have been as patient, and God knew that. I get sick when I think how long and how bad the situation would have been had Travis not been there for her. I have never seen a friend like Travis. Rachel talked to him for a long time … It's okay. Still wish it were me … Am I jealous maybe? Not really. If she can escape from her pain by talking to Travis, it's okay. She feels hate for Shawn. I'm so glad. She doesn't want to go to school. She feels awkward being with friends. I told her it's okay and good to feel hate and anger. She feels bad since God doesn't want us to hate.

I read articles about Rachel's homeroom teacher, about the sexual abuse and how he controlled people. I am so scared of what is yet to come. I am now realizing just what a long hard road is ahead of us. I started to let go. I cried my guts out. I hate Shawn for the first time. I'm glad … I had to let it out. I read Psalm 22. It was written for my pain. How could Isaiah know my pain? I am so thirsty. My throat is so dry. I can't swallow. Ray helped me calm down, but it hurts so much. Ray and I have been so busy and tired … We haven't really let go to come together … He is holding back.

I realize this case is going to be huge. The school was wrong to have kept Shawn in school. The incident that was included in the hearing report on November 3 was a violent attack. He should never have been kept in school. [During the hearing, it was reported that my friend Amanda was dry raped by Shawn in front of her history classroom. As mentioned previously, the teacher was too scared to intervene but did eventually report the incident to the principal. Shawn had a five-day suspension.] *The school should be responsible for keeping unsafe students away from the other students. How I wish this had never happened and that Rachel could go back to enjoying her teen years. She has been robbed … Can't focus on that. She will heal. She will be whole again. Dear God, we need miracles today …*

Ben and our dog, Sophie, have been a comic relief. Luke hasn't talked to Rachel yet. It is so hard … I'd like to pry him open. I realize he's going through lots of different feelings. We told Abigail last night. She cried so hard. She really wants time to snuggle with me. She is so sweet. Our kids are all so good. Last night we were all in the living room … a room filled with so much love. It felt good.

Need to get a lawyer today.

Looking back, I have very little memory of all that happened during the days following telling my parents that I was raped. I know that I stayed home from school for a few days and just slept. I remember having constant flashbacks of being raped and all the terror they put me through. I was so overwhelmed with these memories, and they didn't make sense to me. I had such a normal, happy life, and then all of a sudden, my life was turned upside down. I couldn't understand why this happened to me and how I didn't remember all this abuse. I didn't understand how I could forget what happened to me and keep walking into their traps.

I felt so ashamed and dirty. *How could I have let my parents down so much? How could I have done such awful things?* I was so terrified of all their threats. *How can I keep my sister Abigail safe?* They said that if I told, they would all take a turn and rape her. I could never let them do that to her! They would tell me what she was wearing, say whom she was talking to at the bus stop, and tell me that they were watching her. I kept thinking that I had to be obedient and loyal and not talk to the police or to my parents.

Abigail: I'm not sure at what point Mom told me about your being raped … I'm guessing it was within the first few days. I don't remember overhearing anything, but I'm sure I did. But I do specifically remember lying in my bed one night and Mom came to tuck me in. Phil, a family friend from church, was over, and I was sent to bed early so the adults could talk. I remember lying there and Mom telling me about a really bad guy named Shawn and that he raped you. I don't remember her explaining what that meant, but I understood. I was sad and angry. I felt embarrassed too. I didn't ever ask you about it or talk about it with you.

Dad: There were a lot of meetings between you and the detectives and counselors that Mom and I weren't privy to. That was one of the hard things for me … not knowing what you were able to tell them that you didn't feel you could share with us.

After a few days, I returned to school. Being there was so difficult for me. The sights and smells of the school, hallway, locker room, and gym scared me, and I often had to leave and go to Regina's office. I was having constant flashbacks and needed to talk to her. I needed her to help me make sense of all my broken pieces of memories. Walking down the hall and seeing people turn and look at me, point, and whisper as I walked by was so difficult. Hearing people shout out at me that I was nothing but a dirty prostitute, a rat, a snitch, and hearing crude comments from Shawn's friends made me want to disappear and hide. *I hate this! I hate this! Why did I have to say anything? I should've been stronger! I can't continue like this! Now everybody knows how dirty I am!* Sitting in class and hearing girls I thought were friends talking about how promiscuous I was, that I wanted it and that I'm lying, made me so mad. I remember my friend Salma sitting next to me in language arts class. I had always admired Salma. She was a beautiful Arabian girl with long, silky black hair and beautiful caramel skin and big brown eyes. She was smart and funny, and I enjoyed her company. My first day back to school after Shawn was arrested, while sitting in class together, she began passing a note around the classroom. When the note landed on my desk, I opened it and read her insulting comments about me. I just sat there in awe. I couldn't believe how my friend could be so mean to me! *Why doesn't she believe me? Why is she saying this about me? She knows I'm not like that! If my own friends don't believe me …* I couldn't stand watching how she became a little ringleader and got other people to believe Shawn and not me! I couldn't believe that my own friend was betraying me!

Rachel Green

February 6, 1994

Mom's journal: "But deliver us from evil ..." Rachel needs to be delivered from the evil secrets that are locked inside her. Things are making more sense now. When I see her tremble, and the blank stares, and the shutdown of communication, I now know that she is dissociating. As awful as it all might be, once it is out, it's behind you and you don't have to be haunted by it. Lord, please let Rachel remember, no matter how terrible the memory is. "Deliver us from evil. Give us this day our daily bread ..." Lord, give us what is needed for today. If she can't unleash her memories today, just give her the necessary things to start. Just by putting her wonderful friends in her life right now, you've provided what she needed for that day. You are helping to lay a solid foundation for her for when you finally unleash the memories. She will need the support and love of her friends. Oh, what wonderful friends you have given her! The things that have happened to Rachel have given us so many wonderful opportunities to sit down and really talk. Your glory is being proclaimed. I haven't talked about God to so many friends and people ... It's almost scary how You have used this awful thing that happened to Rachel to bring so much glory to You. Even before this ordeal is all over and we see how things turn out, Your glory is being revealed each step of the way.

And dear Travis—how You provided Travis to Rachel. He was part of her daily bread. He helped us get Rachel back. I will never be able to thank God enough for that blessing. I can't even let myself think about what would have happened if Travis wouldn't have been around. How wide and deep is the love of God. Today, Lord, I have a handle on the situation. I can see so many things in such a clear way. The glory of the Lord shall be revealed.

One thought before I close ... It's as if I found a new dimension of Rachel, and I like what I see. It will be wonderful having this girl who wants to talk about a lot of things. I have to help her use those keys to unlock little doors of everyday happenings. She has always kept so much inside of her. We will work at unlocking little doors. Rachel is so neat, and I'm going to enjoy getting to really know her.

February 7, 1994

Dad's notes: That evening around 11:00 p.m., Rachel was on her bed weeping softly and feeling depressed. All of a sudden, she began to shake. Her whole body shook, making the bed shake. We got very scared and called Regina at home. Regina tried to comfort Rachel over the phone, but Rachel was unresponsive. We decided to call Travis since she felt safe talking to him. After Travis had talked to Rachel for a while, the trembling stopped and she started talking to him. Travis then talked to me and told me about Rachel's flashback and about the second rape.

Mom's journal: It was as if the forces of God were doing battle against Satan in Rachel's body. Her whole body shook. It was Rachel... but not really Rachel ... in such agony. We are totally helpless. We called Regina. Didn't work ... Called Travis. He was the hero. Praise the Lord that Rachel is back! We pray with only groans. I can't think. I can't breathe or swallow. Ray is praying and crying. We have to help her. We feel so helpless, but by God, although she may have gone through it alone, she doesn't have to remember it alone. We reassure Rachel we will walk through the door with her. She talks to Travis, my knight in shining armor. He will always be on a pedestal in my mind. The trembling is finally over. Rachel can talk now. She says it's okay for Travis to tell us about her flashback. She is at peace, exhausted as if she just ran the longest and hardest race. No, that doesn't even compare ... I look at her now. She is holding both stuffed puppies from Travis. She is peaceful. She has remembered. We even joked a little. She asked us why we prayed that she would remember so much. It's easier if it's just forgotten. I told her it was no wonder she remembered so much with all the specific prayers. What a testimony of the power of prayer. What a blessing for her to feel so peaceful after being so tormented. I can't dwell on Shawn ... I would go crazy. Could the power of prayer make him change? Lord, during this flashback, I really thought that You had pushed Rachel and me to the limits. I know You won't give us more than we can bear, but I felt like it! I never drink alcohol, but tonight I did mix myself a drink of OJ and vodka ... I'm exhausted!

Mom: Back in late January, right before Rachel told about being raped, I had noticed Rachel having a bruise on her face and jaw. I thought it was a bruise, but then decided it must just be a dirt smudge or a shadow. At the time, I didn't think much about it. I kept thinking that she wouldn't still have bruises from December 13. I didn't know at that time that she was raped more than once ... Now I realize that I had seen bruises from the rape that took place during the Saturday morning practice.

February 8, 1994

Mom's journal: Praise God for His many blessings. The love and support that was felt today at church was overwhelming. The Baileys brought food, and I felt like angels were really taking care of all our needs. Diana, Jenna, and Ana came to church with Rachel. That was really helpful for her. Ray's sermon was from the heart ... It was very comforting and powerful. Travis came over for pizza. What a wonderful person! Thank you, Lord, for this weekend so we could regroup, feel loved and supported, and be able to request prayers. I feel so confident that You will receive so much glory through this ordeal. Lord, I feel sorry for Shawn because of what he is missing. He may have temporarily taken the life out of our bodies, and his actions certainly have had an effect on us all that will last a lifetime, but he has probably never had the peace in his life that only You *can provide.*

I called Dr. Schroeder to get the test results of Rachel's blood work and to hear his findings during her exam. He said that her report was missing and that he'd call when he found it. I was worried about Rachel having an STD, but he assured me that since she and Shawn are both so young and that Rachel started taking the medicine to prevent diseases, she's probably fine.

February 9, 1994

Mom: While folding laundry, I found a pair of Rachel's panties that had an unusual hole. They weren't torn along a seam or in a manner that could be easily explained. The hole was a straight cut in the crotch area of the panties. It didn't make sense to either Dad or me since it seemed that the hole was made with a scissors or a knife. This was before we knew anything about a knife being involved ... Rachel and I talked, and I asked her about the underwear. She turned away from me and just cried ... She couldn't talk about it. I asked her where they came from, and she said they were in her gym locker and that she didn't know when she brought them home. I asked if she was cut in her vaginal area, and she said no, but that she had a cut on her thigh and shoulder. She showed me her cuts, which were now scars. After talking to Rachel and finding out that a knife had been used in one of the rapes, and especially after seeing the cut in her panties, I made an appointment for Rachel to see our pediatrician. He determined that the cuts were made with a sharp object, the cut on her thigh was six centimeters long, had occurred four to six weeks ago and that the cut on her shoulder was a puncture wound. When I was with Rachel in the exam room and she had to pull down her pants while lying down on the examining table, she began to shake and had such a frightened stare on her face with tears in her eyes. I tried to reassure her, and the doctor said he didn't blame her for feeling that way. The scars that Rachel has on the inside cannot be measured so easily and certainly will not heal as quickly and completely as the scars made with a knife on the outside.

Mom's journal: It's 1:00 a.m. Lord, tonight I come before You trembling. Tonight we experienced the tremendous power of prayer working. You have allowed Rachel to open her memory to remember. We have all prayed specifically for that to happen. Right now I just want to marvel at that miracle, but now that that door has been opened, help us all, Lord, to walk through that door. Do not be afraid of tomorrow—God is already there. *I need to confidently believe and trust and cling to Your promises. You have to provide Ray and me with our daily bread. Our daily bread today will be to be the parents that Rachel needs today to help her the best. We don't want to damage her anymore by what we say, don't say, or by our reactions. You will need to fill us with those skills. Help Travis, Regina, and Dr. McConnell to be the best friends and counselors that they need to be. Lord, each day is its own day ... full of its blessings, happiness, trials, struggles. Each day we have found an oasis from the pain. Rachel was happy today*

Rachel Green

and had a good day. Lord, let us feel your power and presence today. Help us to all get a good rest today. Let us sleep knowing that we rest our heart and lives in Your hands. Thank you, Lord, for hearing my prayer and for answering so many.

Chapter 15

In my mind, I kept hearing Coach Carl yelling at me that I'm worthless and a piece of garbage and that I'm nothing. *He's right. I'm nothing. I'm just a dirty, worthless, crazy girl. Why would my family still love me? I don't deserve to be loved.*

I became depressed and suicidal. I never wanted to actually kill myself; I just didn't know how to live with these horrible memories. I didn't know how to cope with all the insults from the kids at school. It was so devastating to hear what they were all saying, especially when it came from people I cared about and trusted. I couldn't sleep without having flashbacks of being raped. The only way I could fall asleep was to wrap a belt around my neck and hold it tightly until I passed out. I realize this was very dangerous and not a healthy way to cope, but at that moment, that was how I survived. That was the only way I could escape my memories. I would have memories of being raped by Shawn and Sebastian and being yelled at by Coach Carl. Then I would suddenly have flashbacks of when I was only five years old:

> *The monster and his friend screamed at me, "You're such a naughty little girl. Your parents don't want you anymore! You're just a piece of garbage." They threw my little body into the garbage/ compost pile. "You're just a pile of trash. You're so dirty that I'll need to scrub my hands clean. You're so dirty and naughty that I can't even stand looking at you! No one could ever love you since you're so bad."*

Since I didn't have any memories of my childhood before sixth grade, having these flashbacks of when I was a little girl terrified and confused me. *What are these flashbacks about? Am I going insane? Looking at the picture albums and hearing my family talk about their favorite memories, this doesn't make sense. Didn't I have a normal, happy childhood? No one has ever mentioned that I might have been hurt as a child. Why do I keep having these flashbacks of being yelled at and hurt as a young child? Who is this monster in my memories? Where am I? These flashbacks must just be nightmares ... It doesn't make any sense!* I was so confused that I didn't mention these young child memories to my parents. *They'd just think I was crazy or making up stories to get attention.* As much as I tried to dismiss these flashbacks as just nightmares, they kept popping up and grew with intensity.

> *"You're a naughty little girl! You're so dirty and naughty that you're going to be alligator bait!" I was shoved into a tiny wire cage and had a skinned rabbit placed on me since that was what "gators like to eat." The cage with me in it was thrown into the swamp ... The black water soon engulfed my trapped body. I couldn't breathe. My throat felt as if it was on fire, and I kept grasping for anything to hold on to. Everything was black ...*
>
> *"You're such a naughty girl. Your parents don't want you anymore. They told me to get rid of you! Nobody loves you. You're such a bad girl!"*

My entire life as I knew it was just tipped upside down. I began to question everything that I thought was true. *Are Mom and Dad really my parents? Am I really Rachel? Has my entire life been a lie? Why don't I remember anything about my childhood? Why don't I remember my best friend in school? What school did I even go to? What is wrong with me? Coach Carl is right ... I'm just messed up, and nobody would believe me! I don't even know what to believe! I can't handle this anymore! I'm being flooded with horrible intense flashbacks. I feel as if I'm being buried alive in an avalanche of horror. As soon as I try to dig my way out of this mess,* the weight of the terror pushes me back down. I'm buried so deep that I can't breathe or dig my way out.

February 11, 1994

Mom's journal: 11:00 p.m. Today we went to the prosecuting attorney's office to file more charges. How I wish the rapes had not happened! When and where will this all end? Will it be a big ugly case? I keep thinking that maybe if I forget about it, it will just go away. I feel so cheated when I look around at all the other high school kids and think of what they don't have to deal with. Rachel's life was so fun and exciting before the rape—why did this have to happen? Oh, sure, I see so many good things and blessings since then, but why do we have to be tested like this? I can't dwell on those questions ...

Thank you for the good day. Luke had his district swim meet and Rachel and Travis came along. It's always so nice to have Travis around. Tonight a family friend took Luke out for supper. We are hoping that Luke will express his feelings ... We don't have a clue what he is thinking about.

I am so tired!

February 12, 1994

Mom's journal: It's 9:00 a.m. God, I need a jump-start today to get going. All I want to do is sit and stare. It is so hard to breathe. I inhale but can't exhale. There is so much to deal with. Rachel woke up at 4:00 a.m. with a bad headache and keeps remembering falling down stairs. I need to search her room. I haven't seen her green jeans or the matching shirt we got her for her birthday. God, give me the strength just for today to do what I have to do to be the best mom and wife, just for today. I'm exhausted in every way. I'm glad my cold is finally better. I plan on calling Mom today. That will take a lot of energy.

February 16, 1994

Mom's journal: I feel full of doubts, doubting everything I have ever done as a mother. I feel that I made poor choices raising the kids. I feel that maybe I did something to bring this onto our family. It is hard to trust. It is hard to trust you, Lord. When we took the call here, we trusted you. We put our family's life in your hands. There are wonderful people here, but always a struggle. Now this has happened. I feel as if we must be dumb people. How did we get in this situation?

Things are okay today for Rachel—but rape sure destroys so much in one's life!

Chapter 16

While sitting in our squads for gym class, my friend Amanda and I talked. We both were in the same boat, both being terrorized by Shawn and Sebastian. She was in foster care and had a long history of abuse. When I first met her, I thought I could save her and help her with her issues. I didn't understand where she was coming from at first, but when basketball started, I quickly understood her. I understood what she meant when she said that you'll do whatever it takes in order to survive. The more I was hurt and terrorized, the more I leaned on Amanda for support and ideas. Looking back, I should have realized that she probably didn't have the healthiest ideas for coping with life's difficulties. She showed me her arms where she cut herself. She talked about how cutting herself was her best therapy. I was desperate, so I began to do self-harm.

At first, I just scratched myself with anything I could find: paper clips, pen caps, pieces of plastic, little wires, and ends of pencils without erasers. I never cut myself with a knife or razor blade since my goal wasn't to kill myself. Instead, my goal was just to feel something. I was walking around in such a daze, and my whole body and mind were numb. I couldn't tell if I was dreaming or actually awake.

I remember the first scratch. I went downstairs to my dad's office to talk to him. While sitting on the old orange loveseat and talking to him, my eyes were drawn to the blue Bic pen cap lying on his desk. Dad and I kept talking, but I couldn't take my eyes off that pen cap. The phone rang, and Dad turned around to answer it. I quickly grabbed it and ran upstairs, almost giggling with excited nervousness. Now that I had the pen cap, my scratching tool, I didn't know what to do with it. Amanda and I had talked about self-harm as well as how to do it, but now that I had my first tool in my hands, I got scared.

I went to my bedroom and sat on my bed, just looking at it in my hand. I pulled my pants down a little so that I could see my bare skin on my right hip. I thought this would be a good place to scratch myself since no one would be able to see it. I knew it wouldn't kill me if I scratched myself, but as I picked it up and held it above my bare hip, my hand started to shake. I finally made the first scratch. I couldn't feel anything, so I did it again in the same spot with a little more force. It made a pink line that looked like a rug burn. I got excited when I saw the red mark and did it again and again and again, each time with more and more force. Before I knew it, I had scratched my hip open and I was starting to bleed. I still couldn't feel anything, so I kept scratching myself in the same spot, making the blood bead up quickly. It put me into a trancelike state; I saw that I had cut myself open and that I was bleeding, but I could not stop. I became angrier and angrier with myself since I thought I had somehow allowed myself to be raped. I never allowed myself to cry or feel emotions when remembering all that Shawn, Sebastian, and Coach Carl did to me, so the only way I let out all my pent-up anger and emotions was by harming myself.

I finally stopped scratching myself, and I placed a bunch of Kleenex on my hip to stop the bleeding. I pulled my pants back up to hold the Kleenex in place and went to the bathroom to find a Band-Aid. I couldn't believe that I did it. I couldn't believe that I had hurt myself. I was in disbelief, yet it was exhilarating! I actually felt something! I didn't feel the pain of being scratched open, but I felt angry. It felt so good to feel something, even if it was anger aimed at myself. It felt good that I was able to be in charge of my emotions and that it was me who made me angry. Everything else was out of my control. Everything else was caused by my tormentors. I was always just their mute puppet waiting to be played. I, Rachel, finally did something! I was finally in control of something in my life. It gave me a sense of power that I didn't feel before. After that first scratch, I was hooked.

I began scratching myself more and more and finding other ways to harm myself. I was constantly having flashbacks, and the only reprieve I had from such nightmares was when I focused on thinking about hurting myself and planning how I would do it. I began to obsess about losing weight, and I refused to eat. I didn't care about losing weight; I just wanted to be in control of something. No one could force me to eat, so I was in control of when and what I ate. I would drink so much water that I would throw up. The hunger pangs were another way of doing self-harm; my body ached from not eating, but it felt good being able to feel something.

I know that my parents were busy working, talking with the lawyers and detectives, trying to keep me safe, and taking me to my therapy appointments, but to this day, those weeks are all such a blur.

Dad: I remember Shawn as being a skinny punk kid. My clearest memory is seeing him across the courtroom in juvenile hall for one of the first court appearances when he was locked up in juvie. I was sitting with one of the assistant deputy attorneys assigned to your case. I was there alone since Mom needed to be home with Abigail, Ben, and you. I also remember at least once sitting in our minivan in the parking lot of his apartment building and visualizing him at home with his mother ... having not such good thoughts about him ... fantasizing about having a weapon ... Good thing I didn't!

I slowly began opening up to Dr. McConnell about my memories of when I was a young girl. *Please just make these flashbacks stop! I know they can't be true! We were a normal, happy family until I told about being raped.* As much as I wanted to, I couldn't push the memories down:

"No, Mommy, don't leave me here! Don't leave me here! Come back!" I wanted to yell, but I couldn't. I was so scared, I physically couldn't open my mouth or form any audible words. All I could do was watch my mom drive away. The farther she drove down the road, the further my heart dropped. My hopes and spirit sank until there was nothing left but Dolly. Dolly was the mute, obedient, emotionally detached little girl that the Monster created. As Dolly,

I was so emotionally detached that I never cried, smiled, laughed, or got angry. I was as lifeless as a real doll. The monster had created his masterpiece: a real live doll. Even though I was his real live dolly and never complained, I still felt the extreme sadness and emptiness as Mom drove away. I still felt the paralyzing fear as I smelled the monster coming toward me ...

When I was four years old, my family moved to the Deep South of Georgia. We didn't have any family or friends in this state, and it was a hard adjustment for my family. We moved into a tiny rundown two-room cottage. Even though it was less than desirable and was supposed to be temporary, my parents turned the decapitated cottage shack into a true home. I truly believe that a home is where the heart is and where good memories are formed.

Since this was my dad's first preaching assignment, he was eager to get started and make a difference in people's lives. He worked long hard hours writing the best sermons possible, visiting people and getting to know the culture and ways of the people in the small southern town. Mom stayed home with Luke and me, and she was the young, fun, loving, involved, stay-at-home mom who would be the envy of any child.

We went to the little white church every Sunday as a family and eagerly wanted to be accepted and liked by the new congregation. One older couple in the congregation especially took a liking to my family. The husband was fond of me. He would pick me up, carry me around, and tell everyone that I was his dolly. He was always affectionate and kind to me.

As time went by, my family began to experience some difficulties. My mom had a miscarriage, and the congregation responded with a sigh of relief since now they didn't have to find a new and improved living space for my family. My dad was informed that some of the congregation members were having secret meetings, and he didn't agree with their ideas. Things got tough for Mom and Dad as the pressure built and they felt more and more isolated from the community. A few months later, Mom was able to get pregnant again.

And then it happened. Dad couldn't handle the pressure and stress anymore. He grew depressed, and Mom wanted him to get professional help. Dad refused to get help and pinned his arm to his desk with his army knife. The ambulance came and took him away to a hospital. Mom was in her last trimester of her pregnancy and was left all alone to take care of Luke and me, isolated in the country in the middle of a swamp with an unreliable old car and worried sick about her husband. She wanted to visit Dad in the hospital but didn't want me to see Dad in his present mental state.

Even though Mr. Nelson was part of the group who had secret meetings, he and his wife apologized up and down to my mom. She believed that they were sorry, and she forgave them, the way a good Christian wife should do—or so she thought. The Nelsons offered to help Mom out by watching me while she went to the hospital to visit Dad. Hesitantly, she agreed to let Mrs. Nelson watch me. They formed a plan that Mom would drop Luke off at school and then drop me off at their house. She would pick me up after picking up Luke from school. Mom thought this was the best plan since she was needed at the hospital to help Dad with his therapy and I would be comfortable since I knew the Nelsons. This was the first and only time I would ever have a babysitter.

I don't remember the first time I was dropped off at the Nelsons'. I don't even know how it all began. I just know that it ended up being a horrible experience for me and would forever change my family and me.

I remember driving in the car with my mom to go to the Nelsons' house. I sat in the back seat, and Mom would sing and talk with me. I remember looking out the car door window and going past all the rundown old houses with white chickens roaming free, lots of garbage and broken furniture in the yards, and dogs running free along the road. There were few other cars on the road, and we drove through the countryside. Then we would turn onto a dirt driveway and park in front of their house.

Their home was a brownish-gray little house with an old wooden porch. Mrs. Nelson was involved in the flower club, so there were some brightly colored spots among all the depressing brown and grayish-green colors of the Georgian swamps. I loved her flower gardens. They seemed so out of place since they were the only spots of color. They were so beautiful, even though they were surrounded by an old rundown house and dirt lawn with very little grass.

Mrs. Nelson was supposed to be the one who would watch me. However, right after Mom would drive out of sight, she would bend down, look at me, and hold my chin. She would whisper, "I'm sorry, dear. Be a good girl and do what he says." Then I would hear the quiet thump of his cane and smell him. The smell of alcohol and cigar smoke wafted through the stale humid air. The thumping of his cane would come closer and closer. The smell got stronger and stronger. Then I would hear the old wooden screen door slam closed as he came out onto the porch. Mrs. Nelson would give me one last look over her shoulder as she got into her car and went to her flower club meetings. Then my nightmare began. I was left all alone with him. It was just me and the monster.

Chapter 17

February 21, 1994

*M*om's journal: It's 1:30 a.m. Yesterday was awful. For about an hour, I really felt as if God had left us ... had deserted us. I felt that I was in the deep pit all alone. I felt as if I were slipping down a pipe at a rapid speed and couldn't find a grip hole to hang on to. Ray caught me from slipping deeper down that pipe. Lord, I wasn't prepared for what happened today. We prayed that You would give back Rachel's memory, and you are doing that, but now help us all to process what has happened in a healthy spiritual way. I feel so forsaken. The mental anguish is too great to bear. All these things happened, and You spared Rachel's life, and now with Your healing power, You will give her life back to her. The actual things that happened to Rachel aren't as troubling as what she had to endure mentally. The torture ... Dear God, these people have to be punished for this. If I could ask them just one question, it would be why Rachel? Did you really mean to hurt such an innocent person?

Lord, you have to keep Rachel ever so close to You. Never let her slip away to despair. Keep her focus on You. Deliver her from all the evil that haunts her. Make her stronger each day to endure this test. Reassure her that she doesn't have to figure out all this alone. Let her feel—really feel—our love for her. Let her feel Your presence in each day ... each hour ... every minute.

Lord, continue to give Travis the wisdom and love to be this special friend to Rachel.

Lord, when new information is revealed, help me to not react out of *pure emotion. Help me to be a strong, wise mother. It's okay to cry together. But as Ray said, if someone is drowning, you don't jump in if you can't swim … Rather, you throw the person a life ring.*

Thank you for giving me such a wise husband. Sometimes I don't understand all that he is trying to say because I am too emotional. When I step out of my emotional circle, I can see things more clearly.

Please bless Luke, Abigail, and Ben with an extra dose of patience and understanding. Keep our family close to You and to each other.

February 22, 1994

Mom's journal: Travis called and said that Rachel was suicidal. We took her to the hospital, and there were no drugs in her system. She refused to go to Harmony Mountains Psychiatric Hospital and was not able to be admitted to the hospital. Luke and Rachel were really close tonight. It was great to see them reconnect! Luke was a champ! I'm so exhausted!

February 23, 1994

Mom's journal: Rachel finally cried!

March 2, 1994

Mom's journal: So much great despair, Lord. My heart is so heavy—so much anguish that I don't know if I can bear it. Too much gloom in our life. Tomorrow is the hearing … maybe. Such anguish. This will be a heavy load, this legal battle. Rachel's friend Amanda confided to Rachel that she had been gang-raped last May and that she never told anyone. Lord, pain is all around me. I can't see any rays of sunshine today. I only see great pain and so much suffering. Last night Ray visited Mrs. Philips. She told him she had been raped fifty years ago and never told her husband or anyone. Lord, why is this all happening to us? What do you want from us? I feel as if you are putting out a great opportunity to share our experiences and faith, but I can't do it. I'm too exhausted and too sad. Tonight my heart is especially heavy since Travis is going to tell his mom that his sister had been raped.

Lord, I'm totally counting on You to be there for Travis and his mom in this great time of need. Lord, I believe You gave Travis to Rachel during her crisis ... Lord, I'm pleading with you to ease the pain for Travis ... Let his mom be open and warm and show love. Lord, Travis needs so much love from You—and so do Amanda and Rachel. Lord, we need a miracle tomorrow. Please give us just a tiny sign that there will be life after this mess. Rachel sees Dr. McConnell tomorrow. Help Rachel to be open. Help us all tomorrow. It will be a hard day, but we know You will be there with us.

I can't imagine the pain my parents experienced to know that their daughter had been raped and knowing that they had to remain strong and keep life as normal as possible for my younger sister and brother. My aunt Gina flew out to support our family and help out wherever she could. They did an amazing job of supporting me, dealing with all the legal issues, maintaining their jobs as much as possible, and maintaining a sense of safety and security for the whole family.

Once I started reporting being raped, the death threats began and became a daily occurrence. We would get death threats over the phone. They would drive by in the old black van with their guns pointing out the windows at our house and leave "presents" with threatening notes attached to them at our doorstep. When I opened my locker at school, I was often welcomed with hateful threatening notes and even a dead rat in a shoebox with an attached note saying that I was going to die for being a snitching rat. I was constantly told that if I continued to talk to the police, my little sister, Abigail, and little brother, Ben, were going to be killed.

Being bombarded with flashbacks of being raped and ridiculed, having daily death threats, having confusing flashbacks of my being a young child, and being told that I would be responsible for Abigail's and Ben's deaths, I grew more and more depressed and became more and more isolated. I just remember being so tired all the time and being terrified to close my eyes and fall asleep, afraid that if I slept, I would be tormented with vivid memories, that I would wake up and find myself being tortured by them or wake up and find that all my siblings were dead.

Since I wasn't able to concentrate at school anymore and my days were spent going to therapy appointments, talking to detectives and lawyers, and writing in my journal, I dropped out of school. I was sad about not being at school since I loved school and being able to learn and challenge myself, but I was just too terrified and emotionally unfit to attend school. I missed being with my friends and having "normal" things to think about. Thankfully, my friends Jenna, Ana, and Travis continued to be my friends and spent a lot of time at my house. They would fill me in with what was happening at school and just talk about normal things. We would often play Pictionary and other games with my mom and Abigail. It was so nice and helpful to be able to laugh and have fun—even though it was kind of weird that my high school friends and I were playing games with my mom and little sister.

March 5, 1994

Travis was overwhelmed with all the memories I shared with him. He was having a difficult time dealing with his own sister's rape and was becoming depressed. I was told that we couldn't talk to each other anymore, and I was devastated. He was my life string. He was my savior. I felt that it was all my fault that he was depressed and suicidal.

March 9, 1994

Mom's journal: It's 2:30 a.m. I am in total awe of You, Lord. You have answered prayers in abundance. Rachel is such a unique, deep, thoughtful, caring, smart person. I almost come close to saying, "Thank God for the rapes." Lord, You have let this terrible tragedy be the key that is unlocking so many beautiful rooms. I don't know if we would ever have seen these rooms had Rachel not been raped. We talked for hours ... I'm more exhausted now than ever before! I don't want to forget any of the topics we talked about because it was too wonderful. She was so open and honest with me! We talked about her feeling inadequate and not fitting in with the family, being jealous of Luke and Abigail, the special time she had with Ray at Denny's, her dreams of being a vet, life in the parsonage, and hating the times people take away from our time with her dad. The biggest revelation was that Rachel hated God more than she hated Shawn for allowing this to happen. Rachel felt so guilty and bad for hating God. A big change occurred, and Rachel felt God's power after she talked to Regina, when Regina told Rachel she couldn't talk to Travis. Rachel felt so desperate—no reason to live—but she talked about feeling as if she were in a coma and just woke up. She got off the phone with Regina and just knew that it was going to be okay, but that she had to get away from here. She still feels hate toward God, but yesterday, when Grandma, Grandpa, Aunt Gina, Rachel, and I talked, we were able to witness her deep faith. How I wish I could put this all into words. So much has happened that I can't begin to comprehend it all. So many people are praying, and so many prayers are being answered. Lord, I cannot comprehend it all.

March 16, 1994

Mom's journal: Today is the hearing, in thirteen hours. Lord, I pray that your will be done. The prosecuting attorney said it would be an easier case to win if it stays in juvenile court. But then it's off his record once he's an adult. Please, Lord, do whatever is best for Rachel.

March 17, 1994

Mom's journal: The hearing was delayed. The judge wants more information and time.

March 22, 1994

Mom's journal: Okay, God . . . we need a real boost. I am really getting impatient. I'm tired of the rut we are all in. Where is the joy in our life? Rachel has to bear too much. She doesn't know where to turn. Lord, I know she needs to turn her troubles to You, but right now You aren't her friend. You really let her down. We all trusted You with our life—and our life right now is a mess! Lord, you have to give me more patience in bearing this burden and more wisdom in being the mom that Rachel needs. I want to do the best thing for Rachel so do I tell her everything or do I hold back? The conversation I had with Travis was so good. It was so uplifting. Then, when I talked to Rachel, it didn't go so well. She was hurt and is hurting big time. I told her about Travis taking pills and attempting suicide. Too much for all of us to deal with.

Ray is hurting. He had an elders' meeting at church tonight. It must be hard for him. We are here because of his call to preach here, but things aren't going so well with the church or with the family. Lord, help us! We need a miracle today.

March 29, 1994

Mom's journal: It's 7:15 a.m. Lord, it is so hard to get out of bed. I am filled with so much grief and sadness. When will that heavy dark cloud lift from our life? Or do we just have to learn to live with it? I feel so much despair. We are out of that first crisis stage, but I don't know if this stage is easier to be in. It is less urgent ... I always felt as if I were waiting for the scary part in the movie. Well, that has been revealed and now what happens? You are ever present in my life ... I don't doubt You—but I do wonder how You are going to get everyone through this mess.

Chapter 18

Over Easter, my family went to a small town along the Pacific Ocean and stayed in the cabin we usually rented. It was peaceful to get away and relax with my family. As peaceful as this trip was, it was a difficult time for me. It seemed as if every little thing would trigger a memory and I would relive all the horrors that happened to me.

My memories were still pretty fragmented and jumbled up, and I felt I was going crazy. I was diagnosed with having PTSD and a dissociative disorder, and I was trying to figure out what was true, not true, how and when everything happened, who all was involved, and just trying to piece together all the empty spaces in my memories. I felt pressured from the police to figure out all the missing parts of my memories and to make sense of all of them, but the more I worked on remembering, the more painful and difficult it was for me. I often pushed myself to the point that I would become suicidal, violent, or dissociate.

While at the cabin, I wanted to work hard on my memories so I could just get it out and move on with my life. The more I allowed myself to look at my memories, the more withdrawn I became, and I would shut my family out. I spent every evening at the cabin silently crying and shaking in terror. I remember being irritated and angry with my family and getting into arguments with my parents. The more they tried to be supportive and loving, the more I would lash out at them. I finally gave in to Dr. McConnell and began journaling to release all my fears and anger:

April 4, 1994

I had an awful dream … Is this just a dream or is it true? I hate this! I hate guys! I hate myself! What's wrong with me? Am I ever going to be normal? Will I ever trust guys again? Will I ever have a boyfriend after this? Why me? I was fine yesterday—why not today? I wish this whole thing with Shawn was just a bad dream and that I could wake up in seventh grade. I wish I could go back to that age and start all over. I feel as if my childhood was taken away from me. I don't want to have to think about adult things. I want to be a kid …

During the day, I would be okay. I remember being at the beach and playing hide-and-seek with Abigail and Ben in the tall grass on the sand dunes. It was a cool, windy day, but when I huddled down among the tall ocean grass and against the sand, I was able to keep warm in the sun. I found a dip in the grassy sand dune and just lay there for a long time while Abigail and Ben looked for me. I remember feeling so peaceful, safe, and removed from the reality of my life. I loved lying there in the warm sun, feeling the breeze on my face, hearing the grass blow in the wind, hearing the constant crashing of the waves, hearing Abigail and Ben laughing and the seagulls cawing. My journal entry that night:

Wow, am I exhausted! Horseback riding was great! My horse even galloped! The leader got mad at me for making my horse gallop since we were supposed to just walk and trot. After yelling at me several times to slow down, she finally gave up since she saw that I had control. What fun! I felt so free! I helped Ben with his fort back at the cabin. We packed our lunches and then went back to the beach. Ben and I built a fort. He helped me carry logs and even helped me put them on top of each other. I didn't think my little brother could do that. He's growing up much too quickly. Ben, Abigail, and I played all day in the sand dunes. I'm able to be a kid again! I would hide and Abigail and Ben would try to find me. I would whistle to give them a clue as to where I was hiding, but I was always on the move. One time they were getting close to me, so I got up and ran, but I tripped and went headfirst down the dune. Abigail said all she saw were my legs; it was as if I were doing a cartwheel. I was scared at first but realized that I only got a scratch by my eye—then I thought it was fun. I had my slippery pants on, so I could run and slide down dunes easily. I feel so young! It feels so good! As I write this, I'm in a little place that I found. It's an area where all the long grass is stomped down, with long grass standing up around me. It's as if I'm in a whole new world … I only hear the ocean and the grass blowing in the wind … I don't have to worry about Sebastian or Shawn.

I would later use this memory as my "safe place." I wrote a poem that night:

My Ocean

How can I explain a hurt
That runs so far and deep inside?
I can laugh and smile,
But the crying doesn't subside.
To me, it's like the ocean,
Which seems so blue and clear,
But when you go down deep
It's full of darkness and fear.
It seems like it goes on forever
That the sadness will never end,
But then you reach the shore of reality,
Which often feels unlike a friend.
But after every ocean, there's a lake
That eventually runs into a stream,
So I pray to God that the pain will lessen,
And maybe then it won't be so extreme.

April 5, 1994

I had awful flashbacks again … I bit the sides of my cheek because I was trying to keep my mouth closed. Shawn said that if I didn't open my mouth, he'd cut my tongue out. I didn't believe he would do that—I didn't even know he had his knife with him—so I refused to open my mouth. But then he brought out his knife … That knife scares me so much!

5:37 a.m.

I had another awful flashback that I was in Mexico with Sebastian. It was dark outside, and we were talking in the street next to the hotel. In the background were lots of voices, and a rat ran past us. Sebastian was mad, and I got a panicky feeling. Sebastian cornered me against the hotel wall … then I woke up, thankfully. There are birds outside my window building a nest, and whenever their wings hit the window, it reminds me of the rats in the streets in Mexico. Everything triggers memories! Can't I ever get a break from this? Will I ever be healed? Will I ever be able to have a normal life? Will I ever be able to sleep peacefully again? Abigail is still sleeping, and I don't hear anyone awake downstairs, so hopefully I can go back to sleep. Ahhh! The birds are being so noisy!

Well, I didn't get to sleep very long. As soon as I closed my eyes, I started having bad dreams again. I could feel myself being punched, kicked, and yelled at. When I woke up, I checked to see my bruises. When I dreamed I was getting hurt, it felt so real … I could feel the sting and everything. I can't believe that I was only dreaming and that I don't have actual bruises.

Dad and I were left alone at the cabin while the others checked out the shops. I lay in bed reading all morning, and it felt so good. I turned the electric blanket on high, heard the rain beating on the window, felt Sophie's soft fur and warm body cuddled next to me, and smelled the French toast Dad was making for breakfast. It was so quiet for once ... Then everyone came back to the cabin. I got angry. I wanted peace and quiet again. Abigail wanted to be with me. I yelled at her. I told her to leave me alone. She looked as if she was going to cry. I feel bad. I feel like yelling right now I'm so mad! I finally dozed off and began thinking about Shawn. Now I'm really mad! I get mad over the littlest things. I hate being grumpy. I want to be left alone. Mom yells at me when I'm angry. I need to show my anger somehow yet not get in trouble. I feel like screaming. What can I do? I need to yell at something. Is it bad to feel so much anger toward Shawn? He's ruining my life. I lost my virginity, lost my trust, lost so-called friends ... He caused so much pain! I can't even put in words all that I have lost because of that stupid jerk Shawn. My stomach hurts ... I can't stand looking at myself. I feel so dirty, ashamed, guilty, and ... what is the word? Unworthy? No, it's as if no matter how clean I may be on the outside, I feel so empty and dirty inside. It's making me so disgusted with myself. I wish I could talk to my friends. I miss Luke. I can't wait until he comes back from Hawaii. He gets back the day after we get back. Can't wait!

April 6, 1994

Mom's journal: Lord, I haven't been worrying about the financial end of this, but I do need to pray about it. We need to be the best stewards of what we have. Is Harmony Mountains Psychiatric Hospital even an option?

Rachel is hurting today. If she could just learn to let go—to share the thoughts that haunt her—she would recover faster. She has been in such agony too long. I wish she could believe me that she could feel better if she was able to talk about it.

Prayer requests: 1. Rachel will be ready to start with a home tutor and get structure back in her life. 2. Rachel can let friends back into her life. 3. Make me strong for the hearing. Give me courage to face whatever lies ahead. Strength to accept it. Patience and confidence in dealing with the legal system. Trust in You, Lord, that you know what is best for Rachel.

April 8, 1994

Today was terrible. I hated it. It was stupid. I don't know if I'm sad, angry, scared, or nervous. I feel numb. I feel as if my spark to live just died. I don't have any will to live. I'm not going to hurt myself, but I don't care to live anymore. I want my problems with Sebastian and Shawn solved, mainly Shawn, though. I won't be able to live through seeing Shawn at the hearing. I'm going to freeze. I'm so scared of him. He still has control over me. I don't want to follow through with this. If he doesn't get charged and is able to walk scot-free, he's going to come after me and kill me. I promised Shawn I wouldn't tell anyone, just so he wouldn't kill me. I wish he would have. It'll kill me if he's able to walk free with no punishment. What if the judge doesn't believe me?

I'm not ready to see Shawn yet. Hate him. Why me? I hate this. I want to yell. I want to run away. I want to get back at Shawn. I'm too scared. He's going to kill me. I have nightmares every night that he's stabbing me, burning the house down, or shooting me. I keep seeing his knife. Its brownish-gray handle is a little larger than a pocketknife. I finally admitted to Mom that I was burned by Shawn. She kept asking what happened to my hair, and even my haircutter asked. Shawn had a yellow lighter and threatened to burn my hair. He started by burning just the ends, but I got scared as it went up my hair and got closer to my face and burned my eyelashes and sparks burned my face. I hate fire. I've never lit a match or touched a lighter ... Why did Shawn even have a lighter? He doesn't smoke ... He dragged me to the last stall in the bathroom and dunked my head in the toilet to make the fire go out. He kept dunking my head and held it down until I started choking and gave in. When I take showers, I feel as if I'm drowning. I'm so scared of water—everything scares me ... When Shawn gets out, he's going to kill me. I'm beginning to not really care if he does kill me. No, I can't think like this ... I'm just so scared. What can I do? Count the days that Shawn will be held and just sit and hope he won't kill me when he gets out? I feel so helpless. He's getting away with so much because of me. Why won't I just open my mouth and tell everything? Why am I trying to protect him? To protect myself? My family? No, I already said too much to save myself from Shawn. I just can't bring myself to say everything. I'm so stupid. I hate myself. I hate Shawn. He scares me so much. I'm too young to die. I want to live. I'm not going to let Shawn rule over me any longer. I'm going to start to gain control over my life again. I'm going to survive this. I'm a survivor *and always will be. I'm a survivor. I'm a survivor. I'm a survivor!*

April 9, 1994

Well, I woke up at 7:45 and couldn't fall back to sleep. Mom got mad that I haven't been taking my "happy pills" the last several days. Why should I? They don't work. I haven't taken any sleeping pills or happy pills ... They remind me of when I tried to OD and kill myself. I feel so out of place. I was always so happy. Now I'm always sad or angry. I hate this. I always thought positive and saw the best of everyone, but now I'm only thinking negative and think the worse of everyone. I used to like trying new things; I was open-minded and voiced my opinions. Now I hate new things and am scared to say how I feel. I always thought no one could ever attack me. I had lots of confidence in myself. I was able to protect myself. I thought I was all this and that and that no one would ever dare mess with me! Sebastian and Shawn threw me off guard. I've never been threatened before ... I don't even know how to react.

I haven't taken off the necklace Luke got me from Hawaii. It reminds me that I'm a survivor. *I'll keep it on as long as I can. Luke also got me black sand from the black sand beach he went to. It's so neat!*

I asked Mom if we could go shopping. She asked me about two months ago, but I've always been too scared. I'm still nervous, but I'm not going to be locked up all the time at home, so I might as well get used to it.

My bedroom door and closets are covered with cards. So many people care about me—what a great feeling! I wish my aunt Gina and aunt Lianne were here. They said they'd come as soon as I ask. I'll wait until the hearing. I'll need them then.

I'm so scared. I don't want to see Shawn. He's going to kill me. I miss being able to talk to Travis. I feel as if a huge part of me is missing. Ben is so cute and makes me laugh … I'm glad I have a little brother! My family is great. Why did I have to be the one to mess up the family? It would be a perfect family without me. I keep messing up. I cause my family so much grief. I don't deserve such a good family. I deserved to be raped. I deserve so much worse. I shouldn't have been alone or tried to fight back. I shouldn't have told. He's going to kill me. He said if I tell, he'll find a way to kill my family and me. I've never been so scared. What can I do? Nothing. Why do I have to keep being the victim over and over again? Once was hard enough. Ahhh, I hate that victim *word!*

April 11, 1994

I just got back from visiting Harmony Mountains Psychiatric Hospital. It's better than I thought. I don't like the sign. It makes me feel like a mental case. I don't like the doors. They make me feel imprisoned. Nice people, though. I didn't like the smell—yuck! It was a pretty setup, and everything the lady said is what I've been wanting. It sounds okay, but I hate the name. I promised to go there with an open mind, and I did. I actually like it there … I'll never admit it to Mom and Dad, though! I wish it weren't so expensive. I think I could benefit from it a lot. Change the name, smell, and doors, then I'll go! Just kidding. I'll think about it.

April 12, 1994

Ahhh, my dad. I'm so angry. I yelled at him. I feel good and bad. I'm glad I got my feelings out, but I hate yelling at him. I've been so out of it the entire day. I feel so unlovable. I'll never get married. Maybe I wasn't abused by Shawn—maybe my memory is just messed up. Even if I was hurt by him, I wasn't abused as much as others I know. I'm so ugly. I probably deserved it. If I get too close to someone, they're going to find out I'm no good. I'm better off alone—then I won't bother anyone. I'm always in the way, making someone angry. I'm the cause of Shawn hurting me. I could've stopped him. I should've walked away ... I don't need help. It's my problem, and I should be able to take care of it myself. What Shawn did isn't important ... I'm not important anymore. This is affecting me now. Why can't I handle it like before I told? I'm so dirty. I must've led him on. Why do I have to make such a big deal about what happened? I'm just oversensitive. It didn't happen. I'm just crazy. I can't believe it myself ... I must have consented to it by not fighting back. Maybe he didn't mean to hurt me. I just went too far and got him mad. It's my fault I got hurt. I'm so scared. I don't want to go through with this trial. He's going to hurt me, Travis, my friends, family ... Why do I have to mess up so much? This isn't only affecting me, but so many others as well! I feel awful. I hate this. I'm never going to be normal. I don't feel much like a survivor. I hate this. I hate this. I hate this!

April 13, 1994

I had a good day but felt sad, lonely, and robbed. I had fun today, but something was missing—not sure what. I feel sick. I'm so scared. I feel out of control. I'm angry. I'm sad. I want to throw up. I'm so terrified. What's wrong with me? Why did this happen to me? This can't be true. I must be making this all up. It'll just go away ... I hate today. I hate this. I hate Shawn. Hate Coach Carl. Hate basketball. Hate Dad—why didn't he protect me? Hate Luke—why did he say I'm a flirt? Why didn't he take me seriously? Hate Mom and Dad. Hate this ... I hate the word hate. *I just want to forget this all happened. I can't handle this. I'm not strong enough ...*

April 14, 1994

I had awful memories today, but I made it through another day. I really am a survivor!

A poem I wrote sometime in April 1994:

My Nighttime Prayer

I feel like an eagle soaring in the sky,
Now that I realize what has happened to me
And stopped questioning God with, "Why?"
Now that I have trusted God, I am free
From all my burdens that I have to bear.
But now I don't have to be alone anymore,
For now I really feel God's tender care,
Not just on the outside, but in my heart's core,
For now I know what God's son, Jesus, bore
For every person—me, you, and even more.
I feel comforted in Christ by knowing that what He has done
Will turn out to be good and that He's still number one!

April 17, 1994

Mom's journal: Two good things happened today. At church, I talked to Elsa, the activity director at the nursing home. She said Rachel can bring our dog, Sophie, and do "pet therapy" with the residents anytime she wants to. Boy, God, when we need a pick-me-up, you sure know when to do it! Great timing!

There was a good article in the newspaper about dissociation ... It helps to explain things, and I understand better.

Rachel is calling Travis too much. Travis is important in her life, but she doesn't have enough self-control to know how much information is too much. That is where we as parents should step in and help. Ray is afraid to make suggestions for fear of being shot down, and I'm too emotionally involved to make a clear judgment call. Travis's mom is upset with the calling—no more calls allowed. That blow came hard to Rachel ... Thankful that Grandma and Grandpa are here to help with the transition from lots of phone calls to none. Lord, help me to have more insight and wisdom ... Help me to be the best mom I can be for her.

April 18, 1994

I didn't get to see Dr. McConnell today. I was really looking forward to talking with her. I'm quite disappointed. Oh well. At least I have another appointment scheduled in a few days. My grandparents, Mom, Ben, and I went to a large and beautiful dairy farm several hours away. It was so pretty! I loved the calves as they would suck my thumb. They're so soft and cute! Grandpa told me all about his farming days and how different it was back then. It was very interesting. I love the smell of a barn. I was feeling pretty low until I stepped into the calving barn. I smelled the calves, and it reminded me of Grandpa's barn. I think cows are my favorite animal. People make fun of me for that, but I don't care. When I was in the sixth grade, I drew my future plans, but now I can't find them. I want to make Grandpa's barn into an indoor riding arena; board horses; be a vet; be a counselor; train dogs, and have cows, goats, dogs, cats, horses, and llamas. I know it's impossible, but that's my dream. I don't want to be rich, just be able to pay taxes and such. I want to help people and make them happy. I want to help animals that are hurt, have my own farm, be married to a loving non-abusive husband, and still have trust in God and have a strong faith and stay close to my family and friends. I'm not sure what I want to be more—a vet or a counselor. I love animals, but I really want to help abused children. Maybe I can have a counseling office on my little farm ... That way I can be with animals and at the same time help others. I have so much going for me ... How could I even think of ending it so early? I have a good life ahead of me, and I'm going to see it, for I'm going to live through this. I'm a survivor. I'm going to accomplish some of my dreams—just you wait and see!

It's 2:23 a.m. I woke up gagging. I hate Shawn. Why did I get him so mad? Why did I tell? I could feel him choking me ... Now my throat hurts and I keep thinking about him. Well, it's now 2:27 a.m., so I'll try to forget and fall back to sleep. I'll try hard. I'm strong ... I can beat this!

April 19, 1994

I slept terribly. I woke up several times and had awful memories. These memories are new and very confusing ... I hate them. I was blindfolded ... Someone else was with me—not Shawn or Sebastian ... I was forced to drink orange juice ... Coach Carl? No, it can't be. Why would my coach do this to me? I was kicked in the ribs and stomach. Who are these men? This can't be true!

I yelled at my mom today. She took all my stuffed animals so she could do a complete cleaning. She teased me and said she was going to give them to Goodwill. I didn't know she was teasing, and I felt as if I had nothing ... as if everything was being taken away from me. I feel as if I have nothing left of my old happy life. I just want to hold on to something from my life from when I was happy and carefree. I need something to hold on to give me hope that life will someday return to normal. I can't believe that I yelled at Mom for something so dumb—it's not as if I've played with my stuffed animals recently!

I went on a walk with Mom. We had a nice talk. I told her that I wanted to yell at Grandma. I got in an argument the first day they came. I'm so angry with her for blaming the rape on me when she first heard the news ... I'm so angry at her, but I love her. She says she doesn't think that anymore, but it still hurts. I'm doing a lot of faking around Grandma.

April 27, 1994

I'm so angry at Coach Carl! At the Jefferson game, he said there would be a basketball practice the next day. He cancelled the practice, and I was the only one who didn't know. He set me up to get raped! My coach set me up and he raped me! Who can I trust? Who will even believe me? And my homeroom teacher ... No wonder I was happy when he was killed!

April 28, 1994

Coach Carl, I'm so angry at you! I don't understand why you hurt me so much. First, the pain of realizing that someone hurt me—a coach, *for crying out loud! You are a terrible man ... You should never have been called coach. I respected you ... the way coaches should be respected. I did whatever you wanted, I tried your new basketball techniques, I never questioned you, I looked past my anger toward you and kept giving you a new chance ... But what did I receive from you? Oh, I got a lot from you—always being put down, hit if I did your techniques wrong, set up to get hurt, treated like a toy, and worked like a robot.*

Second, the pain of living and knowing that I'm no longer a virgin. How could you rape me? Why did you set me up and hold me down? What did you have against me? You invaded my privacy. You completely changed my life and so many others' in an awful way.

Third, the pain of all the physical abuse. I hurt so much. You screwed up my ankle and knee. I can't even run a mile without my knee swelling up. My face still stings at the thought of you hitting my face. I have to daily remember the knife cuts from you as I look at the awful scars on my body.

Fourth, the emotional pain. You said I was worth nothing, I'm no good, I'm stupid, I have no rights, I was born to be "used," I deserved it, I'm only good for sex, and all the other sayings you said to me. I believed all your lies. You made me into a robot. That's not right. You're a coach ... a teacher ... an adult ... You're supposed to build me up, not tear me apart!

I'm no longer your victim!

After several days of extremely difficult flashbacks and constant triggers, I was able to put together more pieces of the puzzle. I remembered that Coach Carl and the others were involved in raping me. When I first thought that it was only Shawn and Sebastian, it was scary, but now that I knew that Coach Carl, my homeroom teacher, Detective Clark, and the "doctor" were involved, I was terrified out of my mind. Shawn and Sebastian were just teens like me, but these men were respected, trusted adults who had connections. This was way out of my league.

When I first began telling the detectives that others were involved, they had a difficult time believing me. When I started to give them more details and information, it was obvious that something changed for them, for they quickly asked more questions and began scribbling notes. The two detectives kept glancing at each other while writing in their notepads. When I finished talking, they told me that I need to be very careful not to mention some names ever again. They said that if I ever mentioned his name, it would be very serious for my family and me. They told me that this case was too complicated for them to handle and that I needed to drop the case.

When my parents were finally allowed back in the room with me, the detectives told my parents that I needed to stop changing my story. I was furious with the detectives. I wasn't changing my story. I was just remembering more and more of what happened to me. I can't help it that I mentioned some "big names" to them. In addition to not changing my story, I wasn't purposefully withholding information. These detectives were intimidating, insensitive, and infuriating. When they finally left, I had little to no trust in law enforcement.

As soon as word was out that I remembered Coach Carl being involved in raping me, the death threats were more common and more threatening. My family had to board up the windows in fear that we would be seen and shot. When going past windows that weren't covered up with boards, my family had to crawl and remain below the window frame in order to not be seen. All of our phone calls were being recorded and monitored by the police, but all the threatening calls came from unlisted numbers and ended before they could be traced. When going to my therapy appointments or meetings with our lawyer, I had to hide in the car. Living like this was terrifying, yet through it all, my younger siblings seemed unaffected. Abigail made it into a game with Ben to see who could crawl the lowest and fastest past the windows. Mom and Dad were able to hide their fear and panic and keep making them feel that life was normal.

Abigail: Life changed drastically after you began telling. We eventually started to stay home from school. I remember Phil and his wife being over a lot; not sure if they were watching Ben and me or what. Then the threats began … Ben and I made it a game to always crawl under the window so we wouldn't be seen. I remember seeing a black van circling our block. We couldn't go outside to play. I think that because of my young age of ten, I never felt scared. It was actually kind of fun to be on lockdown in our home; Ben and I played a lot in my room. I don't really remember things being explained to me, yet I had an understanding of what was going on.

For their safety, Luke, Abigail, and Ben were sent to live in Wyoming with my relatives. Luke, being a junior in high school, was understandably angry about having to leave his friends and his life. Abigail, at the young age of ten, innately became the mother figure for Ben and was very brave and understanding. Ben, who was only five, was too young to understand or even to know the dangers we all faced. I can't even imagine the heartache my parents felt as they dropped them off at the airport and had to say good-bye.

Abigail: I don't remember if we were told the night before that we were going to Wyoming or not. But I remember being woken up in the early morning—felt like the middle of the night—and being taken to the airport with Luke and Ben. They said we were going to spend time with Grandpa and Grandma. Luke was quiet and Ben cried a lot, so I made it my job to cheer him up and keep him happy. I was excited since it was my first time on an airplane. I don't remember saying good-bye to Mom, Dad, or you. We got to go in the cockpit and meet the pilot. I felt so grown-up and cool since we were flying by ourselves. The flight attendants flirted with Luke and thought he was our uncle! I'm not sure how long it was that we were in Wyoming, but eventually Aunt Gina insisted that we go to school. I think there was only a week or two left of fourth grade. I was so scared walking into the new school. There were so many questions about why a new kid would be starting school so late in the year. But honestly, being in Wyoming was fun for me. I loved getting to see Grandpa and Grandma. I loved being in the country. I was with Ben constantly. I was at that age where I was aware of what was going on, but it didn't really bother me or affect me.

Chapter 19

Early May 1994

One evening in the first week of May, I was talking to Travis on the phone. While talking, the phone beeped and I answered call-waiting. Sebastian was on the other line, and he was telling me that I was going to die. He went into detail how they were going to shoot me when I least expected it. He said that I would have to watch my every step since I would never know where they would be hiding and waiting to kill me with their guns. He said they would enjoy killing me but that their ultimate goal would be to catch me alone with Abigail so they could have fun with her and make me watch her get tortured. While listening to these threats, I started screaming at him and hung up the phone. I ran into my dad's office while he was talking to Phil, a dear family friend. Screaming and shaking, I told them what just happened. Phil said, "That's it! You're staying with me and going into hiding."

I don't even remember packing my bag, but I grabbed my duffel bag and went that night with Phil. I had to stay on the floor of his big white truck so that I wouldn't be seen. He took many turns and took the extra long way to get to his house just to make sure no one was following us. When we got to his house, Phil and his wife, Patricia, closed all the blinds and I had to crawl when going past windows. I remember sleeping on an air mattress and watching Phil pace the hallway armed with his gun or quietly keeping watch near me while I slept. I felt protected and safe, but I was angry. I felt like I was letting

Shawn, Sebastian, and everyone else win by scaring me out of my own home. I was angry and confused as to why I couldn't call or contact any of my friends. I felt safe with all the extra caution, but it also made it all that more scary and real. Seeing Phil react like this made it very clear to me how serious the threats were and how much danger my whole family was in.

May 5, 1994

Grr. I hate this. They are going to kill me. Last week I saw their black van drive by my house. My dad is having a meeting with church council. I prayed for him. It's going to be hard for him—he's going to tell them why he's taking a leave of absence and what's been going on. My mom asked me why I was quiet today. I guess it's because I miss Luke, Abigail, and Ben. I'm glad they're away since I would die inside if they were ever hurt. But I have to admit, I really miss them! The whole day I felt like crying. When will I see them again? I wish Shawn would've just killed me. I'm causing my family such hard times. I'm tearing my family apart—just as Coach Carl said. It's my fault I got raped, beaten, and caused my family to have problems. If I didn't tell anyone, my family would be the way it used to be. Dear Lord, please let me see the truth and stay firm in You.

I have mixed feelings right now. Mom and I were playing double solitaire when Aunt Gina came home from the church meeting. I asked how they took the news. I thought they would be angry, but I was wrong. Aunt Gina said there was so much love in the room and that they were all very caring and so sorry. I feel good that they all took it so well. I was really worried about it. Later, after the rest of the meeting, Dad and the district pastor came home. It's kind of weird and scary to know that people in church now know about my being raped and how scared my family is. Aunt Gina is leaving tomorrow :(

May 6, 1994

Mom, Dad, and I are going away until Sunday night. We're going to go on a long hike and go horseback riding. It'll be fun and pretty. Can't wait to get away. I feel like a prisoner. I can't go outside, stand in front of windows, or talk to any of my friends. I wish I could talk to just three people a week. I just want to keep in touch with them and hear what's going on at school and such. I wouldn't talk about the trial—just fun stuff. I want to be normal. I want to see Luke. I miss him. I want to be able to go outside and jog. I haven't talked to Travis for three weeks. I go to bed crying ... I want to talk and see him. I miss having a life, talking to friends, going outside, and jogging. I also miss my siblings. Well, I'm beginning to get sleepy. I had woken up at 4:00 a.m. to say good-bye to Aunt Gina, and the night before, I went to bed at 2:30 a.m. and woke up at 7:00 a.m. It's now 1:20 a.m., and hopefully I'll fall asleep quickly. This is one of the first nights that I'm able to fall asleep with a peaceful feeling. No matter how hard a day it is, God always lets something positive happen. Praise God!

May 7, 1994

Well, today was okay. I slept until noon. Mom and I went outside on the deck at the hotel and got sunburned. It felt sooo good to be outside! It was so peaceful and warm. Dad, Mom, and I walked over to Arby's for lunch—finally something besides pizza or spaghetti! Mom and I went on the deck to enjoy the sun again. All three of us went horseback riding. It was really fun. I really liked the layout of the ranch. Mom and Dad were stressing, and I laughed so hard at them! They had no idea what they were doing.

And now the bad part of the day: we had a talk today. They won't let me see or talk to any of my friends. I have to be with them twenty-four hours a day. I'm so sick of them! I need some space! I want to talk to Jenna, Ana, Travis ... I feel like a prisoner. I can't do anything ... not even go outside by myself!

May 10, 1994

I had a great day! Jenna and Ana came over, and we planned Ana's birthday party. We talked for a long time. It felt sooooo good to talk to someone my own age! We laughed so hard. I felt so normal! I had so much fun. We played Pictionary with my mom. Ana and Mom won, so Jenna and I had to pick up. It was really fun. Ana and Mom are still undefeated. Jenna and I will win soon. :) I feel like singing … I'm so happy. I can't remember when I felt like this. I didn't know that I missed talking to friends so much. I'm actually getting a life back :) (I hope!)

May 11, 1994

I just finished the book Remembering the Good Times, by Richard Peck. What a good book! If you know anyone who is suicidal, have them read this book. This book makes you feel awful for even considering suicide. How could I ever think about killing myself? I'm going to have Amanda read it.

May 12, 1994

I have a lot of feelings right now. I'm not sure how to start or sort them out. I'm mainly scared … terrified. They're going to get me. My ear has been bugging me so much. They're going to kill me. I let the cat out of the bag, and now I'm going to pay for it. My leg is acting up again. It's as if I have no feeling in my left leg … I can't even stand or walk. I feel so frozen. I won't be able to run from them. They will catch me and hurt me. I'm getting out of shape. I can't even run a mile and a half without breathing hard. I used to be able to run two miles easily. How am I ever going to be able to get away if I can't even go outside, get some physical activity, and get back in shape?

I know why I never smiled for pictures … I hate having my picture taken … I hate Georgia! I have a headache. My ear is bugging me. My leg is numb and I feel like crying. I'm so sad. I'm not really sure what I'm sad about. My ankle still hurts from when I hurt it in basketball. It only hurts if I move it in certain ways, like going up stairs or jumping on the trampoline.

I can't wait until Uncle Steve comes. He flies in tomorrow around 5:00 p.m. He's so funny and has jokes and stories to share.

May 13, 1994

Well, so far today is awful. I got in an argument with Mom. I feel sick. I had awful dreams. I kept waking up, and I saw every hour on the clock.

May 14, 1994

Yesterday morning was awful but then turned great. Jenna and Ana came over. We had so much fun! Jenna spent the night, and we stayed up until 3:00 a.m. talking and laughing. Last night we looked through the yearbook, and the first picture I saw was Coach Carl. I let out a scream and dropped the book. I tried to hide my fear, but Jenna was able to see past it; we put the yearbook away. We ended up having a pillow fight, baking cookies, playing pool and basketball, and playing with Sophie outside. It felt so good to be outside!

I'm worried about Ana. Jenna and I stayed up until 3:00 a.m. trying to figure out what we can do about her. I feel so helpless.

I just got back from horseback riding. Uncle Steve, Dad, Mom, and I all went, but Mom and I were the only ones who rode horses. I had fun. I love horses—they make me forget all my problems. It's so quiet there.

On the way to the ranch, I asked when the last time Uncle Steve was here to visit us. They were all surprised that I didn't remember. Uncle Steve, Aunt Cindy, and Aunt Tammy were here last November over my birthday. They also said that the same week they were here, I went to Canada for a soccer exchange for several days. I don't remember any of this ... and it was only one year ago! What else don't I remember?

May 15, 1994

We just got done eating dinner. Mom made roast beef, potatoes, French peas, and pie. It was so good! Uncle Steve prayed after dinner. Everyone started to cry, except me. Not sure why they cried.

I'm going to Jenna's house! I can't believe they're going to let me stay overnight!

I finally know why I feel sad. I'm sad about all that happened to me, but this is a different sadness. I always denied that I liked Travis more than just a friend. When I play the song "I Will Always Love You" on the piano, I get all teary-eyed. My mom said it's a healthy sign if I can feel the feeling of love toward a guy with everything that I went through. I miss him so much.

I had fun at Jenna's house. I really believe my thoughts and concerns about Ana are valid. She shows so many signs of it. I want to be a foster parent and help abused kids. They need a stable home, love, attention, someone who believes in them, and a good role model. My mom should do it ... I think she would be great as a foster parent. My dad has told me he has always wanted to since he also had a difficult life. They both would be great. Mom said she'd like to adopt Amanda and Ana. Whenever they come over, Amanda and Ana hug my mom and always talk to her a lot. Ana always asks Mom to come wherever we go. At first, it bothered me that they would show Mom so much attention. It was as if I was competing against my mom for their attention. A while ago, Mom and I talked about my feelings, and since then it's been great. They still give her hugs and include Mom when we play board games, but Mom knows they're my friends and when to leave us alone. Mom's great.

It's going to be weird to go to our church again. I haven't gone for five Sundays (three because I was "hiding" and two because I was sick and throwing up). I'm scared to see the church council. I haven't seen any of them since my dad told them I was raped. How are they going to react? Mom and Dad keep reassuring me and only show concern and love for me. I'm still scared.

May 15, 1994

I slept terribly and had awful dreams. At first, church was nice. I sat by my dad. I can't remember ever sitting next to him at church since he's always preaching. He said it felt weird to have someone else preach in his church. The sermon was nice and was about saying good-bye and parting from family and friends. Dad and Mom cried. I couldn't see if Uncle Steve did or not. After church, I felt really weird. People kept coming up to me and giving me hugs. Everyone was crying. Everything started to sink in and I started to cry ...

Dear God,

I feel so filthy. Things have happened to me that I wouldn't wish upon my worst enemy. I have done things that make the perverted blush in embarrassment. I feel as if I have been deeply stained and forever dirty. I am damaged beyond repair.

I find that trusting you, real *trust, is difficult for me. If I can't trust people I can see, how can I trust you? Why did you let these things happen to me? Why didn't you rescue me?*

I've been told that you love me. I'd like to believe that, but the word love *is so polluted in my heart that it's hard for me to know what your love for me means. To be quite honest, in some ways, I'm afraid of love ... from you and from others.*

I understand I need love. I need your love. I know I need you to be in my heart, my trembling, wounded, shattered heart. I know that I need to let down my defenses and put your holy healing hand upon me. It's so painful, Lord. It's so awful. I'm so ashamed to even think about what happened. How can you love me? Are you really willing to love me? I hope so, for without your love I will be helpless, lost, and hopeless. Please love me, but be patient with me as I learn the truth about love. Teach me the truth of how your love feels. Please help me to love.

The night of May 15, I was in my brother Luke's room talking to Travis on the phone. I was sitting at Luke's desk and found a knife in his desk drawer. As I was talking to Travis, I picked up Luke's knife and gently traced my vein on my left wrist. I was sharing a memory with Travis and was feeling depressed. I admitted that I found a knife in Luke's desk and that I was holding it. He insisted that I put it away and talk to my parents. I got mad at him and hung up. I took the knife to my wrist and sliced my wrist. As I did this, Travis called back and my mom answered the phone. Travis told my mom that I was suicidal and that I had a knife.

My parents took me to the ER and had my wrist bandaged. The next morning, I had a therapy session and admitted that I was very depressed and scared, and I talked about being suicidal. I was then taken to Harmony Mountains Psychiatric Hospital and put on suicide watch. I hated being at the hospital. I hated that I had to be behind doors that buzzed when they closed and locked me inside. I hated being around other people and having to open up to them about why I was there and what happened to me. I hated the first night being there and being questioned over and over by different doctors and therapists about what brought me here. I kept trying to tell them that I didn't want to die—I just didn't know how to deal with all the stress and memories. I hated the psychological tests they performed; I felt they were trying to scare me or get a reaction out of me. The inkblots that they showed me scared me and triggered memories. I hated how every little thing I said, and how I appeared, was being scrutinized and analyzed. I didn't care if they believed me or not. I just told them all that I could remember as if I were a robot. I knew what happened to me, and if they didn't believe me, then oh well, that was their choice. I had very little faith and trust in anyone. They all said they wanted to help me, but I didn't believe them. Even though I was scared out of my mind about the memories and all the threats, I couldn't feel any emotion. Yes, I knew that all that trauma happened to me, but at the same time, I didn't feel any attachment to the memories.

Even though I hated being at the hospital, I forced myself to be the role model patient so that I could get out of there ASAP! I hid my anger of being there, and I quickly made friends and found myself focused more on helping them than myself. I kept trying to figure out one of the girls in my unit. She thought she was a cat and would spend the whole day sitting on the arm of the couch, licking herself, meowing, or sleeping like a cat. She never talked, just meowed or hissed at people. She was a puzzle for me, and it was my mission to figure her out. The others kept telling me to forget it since she was too crazy, but I kept thinking that we must all be crazy or else we wouldn't be here! As much as I tried to figure her out, I never could.

While at the hospital, I went to the "school" in a different wing of the hospital. Walking to the classrooms was a scary experience for me. We had to pass other units, and I remember being terrified to go past D2, the unit known for housing the most severe cases. When we walked by, they would bang on the door and windows, and they acted like psychotic rabid animals who would tear you apart and eat you without hesitation. I was so thankful not to be on that unit!

When we got to the classrooms, the teachers were nice and it was a most comfortable and relaxing atmosphere. There were a few desks, but otherwise we could sit on couches, comfy chairs, or beanbags. It was such a nice welcomed break from being on the same unit and having to talk about memories. I had been out of school for awhile, so I was eager to learn again. I was quickly disappointed since their materials were all too easy and boring.

While in group one day, one of the girls mentioned being raped. While talking, she slipped and said the name of the rapist and what school she went to. It turned out that she was raped by Juan, Sebastian's older brother. She told me to stay away from Juan and his brother since "they were bad news and messed up." Since the therapist found out that we went to the same high school and that I knew Juan, we were separated and not allowed to be in the same group.

May 21, 1994

Dad: The church synod district president knew a lawyer member in his congregation who got us in touch with the civil lawyer. She was part of a very high-profile legal firm ... Their office downtown was like a scene from a movie. The church loaned us some of the money we needed to pay legal fees. My initial reaction to her and her team was that they were more interested in winning a case than they were about representing or caring for us. That was confirmed for me when before the case ever went to court and you had hurt yourself, they dropped the case and no longer showed any interest ... evidently because they didn't think they could win.

To at least some extent, the same could be said for the ADA. The assistant district attorney seemed to lose interest in the case after you hurt yourself too. I remember her saying something like, "The only credible witness has now become harder to believe." She didn't think she had a case she could win in court.

While all this was going on, the legal team from the school district (their "A team") was doing their best to intimidate us ... and we were sending stuff back and forth by courier to our legal team. The school district legal team was scary. They did their best to intimidate us. We were thankful at that time to have the civil attorney we had hired. I think they could smell blood! Again, it was all like some scene out of a movie. The school district legal team would send us something by courier, we'd have it picked up by our courier and sent to our legal team, and they'd courier something back to us ... This was in the days before e-mail, fax, and instant communication.

When I was at the hospital, the case was dropped and Shawn was released from juvenile detention. His parole officer had overheard him tell another inmate that he was going to pretend he was suicidal so that he would be admitted to the hospital where I was. Shawn told the parole officer that he was going to come after me and kill me. The parole officer contacted my parents, our lawyer, and the detectives. He said he had heard many threats before, but never had he seen or heard someone look so evil and determined to follow through with the threats.

I did not know that such threats were made against me and was completely baffled when a nurse woke me up in the middle of the night and told me to pack my things. All she said was that my mom was coming to pick me up and that I was going to a different hospital. I was so confused. I had no idea what was going on.

Mom came and picked me up, and the taxi dropped us off at the airport. Mom told me we were flying to Dallas to go to a hospital that specialized in treating patients with PTSD. I was so excited to fly, and I loved the adventure. I still had no idea why I had to be swept away in the middle of the night and why we had to be so secretive.

Chapter 20

May 22, 1994
Esperanza Psychiatric Hospital

The taxi dropped us off at the front lobby of Esperanza Psychiatric Hospital in Dallas, Texas. It was a beautiful, spacious campus made up of several different redbrick buildings. I liked this hospital more than Harmony Mountains since it didn't seem or look as institutional. Yes, the doors locked, but I never got the caged-in feeling as I did at Harmony Mountains Psychiatric Hospital. The security devices were much more discreet, and it was much homier.

When I was shown around with my mom, I felt confident and sure of myself. I actually liked the place and found this new place to be an exciting new adventure. As soon as my mom had to leave, reality struck. I was being left at another psychiatric hospital. I thought I'd be able to outsmart the doctors here and trick them into believing that I was "healed" and all better. I was wrong. They were able to see right past my mask, making me angry and wanting to rebel.

Dad: I had to finish up some business at home before driving to Texas, but I remember it being very hot when I drove from our home on the West Coast to Texas. When I finally got to Esperanza, you didn't seem all that excited to see me. I had to deal with my temporary letdown and finally realize that it was pretty petty in the whole scheme of things! I needed to realize that to you in your emotional state, it was no different than if I had driven around the block on an afternoon when I had nothing better to do. Guess I had a lot to learn!

Your therapist had a national reputation as being one of the best for treating patients with PTSD and dissociative disorders. I remember being interviewed by her and feeling as if I were a suspect, but she explained this was just normal procedure and that they had to ask the questions they did. I don't remember any of the specific questions, just that the questions made me feel angry and icky.

The hospital grounds were very pleasant. There was a fairly good sized pond with a water fountain. Several times we sat outside ... you and me and with Mom before she went to Wyoming to be with Luke, Abigail, and Ben. The hospital was only about a twenty-minute drive from New Beginnings ...

A friend I went to college with was the director of New Beginnings, a home for unwed mothers, and offered me a place to stay while in Dallas in exchange for doing devotions and being an on-site spiritual advisor to the girls who were part of the program at New Beginnings. New Beginnings leased part of an older apartment building ... Every couple of steps in that building, you would build up static electricity and would have to touch a wall to ground it or you'd get a real shock when you touched any doorknob. The walls were very dirty. I'm not sure how long I was there—two weeks, maybe. Many thanks to my friend for making the offer ... It saved us from what would have been a costly motel bill!

It was also during this time that I applied for and tried a writing assignment for a Christian publishing company. But given the situation and the stress, I was unable to concentrate; my attempts to write something catchy and new and good came to nothing. The publishing company let me down easily. I was still without a job, however!

For Rachel, her life was being at the hospital and working through memories. She didn't need to be thinking about anything outside of the hospital. For me, there was the rest of the family to also think about and make plans for—where to live, what schools should the kids attend, finding a job, finding new therapists/doctors for Rachel, working with the school district. There was also all the stuff that comes with an interstate move: driver's licenses, insurance forms, change of address, and so on. I was trying *to write for the publishing company and was on call at New Beginnings. Even though it was different from all the tough things that Rachel was going through, it was all a little overwhelming for me. I wanted to be there for Rachel, felt responsible to provide for my entire family, tried to get our life back in order ... and I had no idea how to do it.*

The first few weeks of my stay at Esperanza were very challenging for me and my parents. I was refusing to do any therapy work and began to take out my anger by doing self-harm. My consequence was that I wasn't allowed to leave my building unit, and my visits with my parents were short and minimal. I was enrolled in every imaginable therapy: group therapy, individual therapy, music therapy, movement therapy, art therapy, recreational therapy, and self-esteem therapy. I had never heard of so many different types of therapy and thought it was silly.

I hated music therapy and movement therapy the most since I felt the most threatened with these. I liked the therapists, but I felt uncomfortable and threatened to move in certain ways and to have others invade my personal space. I really enjoyed recreational therapy and art therapy. Larry was the recreational therapist, and our group would climb up high poles to do rope obstacle courses. We had to trust each other and work as a team. I loved the challenges and doing something that seemed dangerous. The bigger the risk, the more willing I was to try it. We would also play sports and do other activities that taught us to trust each other, made us work as a team, and taught us how to cope with difficult situations by using safe and healthy activities. It taught me to channel my frustrations and emotions into sports and other physical activities.

While at Esperanza, I lived for adventure and danger. When my parents visited me and I was finally given a pass to walk outside with them, the adventurous side of me would come out. We'd be out walking and I would run and try hurdling over the signs in the lawn. Mom and Dad got mad and thought I was trying to hurt myself. That was the end of my freedom outside.

Besides seeking adventure and danger, I sought revenge and a way to express my anger. I was bored one day and found a little string on the carpet in my hospital room. I began pulling on it and kept pulling until I had unraveled a small section of the carpet. I showed my roommate, Jessica, what I had done. We both giggled and put on mischievous smiles. I went back to pulling on the string and unraveled a larger section of the carpet, while Jessica used the string to hurt herself by wrapping it around her wrists and ankles so tightly that she began to bleed. I kept working on the carpet throughout the night, only jumping into bed when we heard the nurse coming to check in on us. The sound of the carpet being unraveled was music to my ears! I felt such power by destroying my room. It became almost addictive ... The more I pulled and unraveled, the more ecstatic I became. By the next morning, I had unraveled a large section of the room's carpet. I got bored, so I started to test the outlet with my metal barrette. I didn't get much of a shock, so I decided to dismantle the outlet. Once I had the cover off, I began using my metal barrette to poke around inside the outlet, causing several shocking moments. I then got the great idea that it could probably be a secret passageway between my room and the room adjacent to mine. I put the cover back on and told Jessica my plan. We rearranged our room by moving our beds and desks to cover up the unraveled carpet.

While eating breakfast as a large group in our unit's small kitchen, I quietly told Lindsay, one of the girls who stayed in the adjacent room, my plan. She was all smiles since she was excited to hurt herself in any way and had to wear a helmet to protect her head from being banged into the wall and large white mitts for her hands to prevent self- injury. Since she always had to wear the mitts, we asked her roommate to help us. We decided that during the night, her roommate and I would both dismantle the outlets and see if we could see each other and pass things back and forth through the opening. I had a new mission and I couldn't have been more smug and excited.

We got right to work that night and discovered that my idea worked! We could see each other, but the opening was very small since the wires were in the way. However, it was big enough for stashing the pills that I refused to take!

It didn't take long for the staff to find my piled up carpet string and exposed floor. I was immediately taken to what we patients referred to as "the fishbowl." It consisted of several tiny bare white rooms in our unit, where the back wall of each room was Plexiglas looking into the nurses' station. The only thing in that plain white room was a thin plastic mattress that was literally only an inch thick, a small pillow, and a white sheet. All my privileges were taken away from me, and I couldn't leave that room. I had to stay in there all day except for my individual therapy sessions, using the bathroom, and taking a shower. I never realized how lonely, angry, and bored a person could be while in isolation and being watched twenty-four seven by a nurse on the other side of the Plexiglas. I think that the nurses were as angry and bored as I was, because they would never change facial expressions or even communicate with me. They would just sit there doing paperwork and watch me with the same blank faces as though I weren't even there. Even when it was shift change, the new nurse would look the same as the one who was there for the past twelve hours … except for one nurse who worked one evening while I was in the fishbowl. I never found out her name, but she was a kind woman who actually smiled and would open the Plexiglas window to talk. She had a gentle and cheery voice, and she even gave me a deck of cards with which to amuse myself.

Mom's journal dated May 24: It's 11:30. Dr. Shey called. Rachel is in seclusion because she needs to be safe. She needs to connect and refocus and write down why she is feeling angry. It is a power struggle right now. She won't talk to Dr. Shey, but she was able to tell them she hurt herself with a Tic Tac box and that she destroyed her room. I can visit her at 1:15. I need to reinforce being honest and keep things out of her room that can harm her. I need to reinforce that she needs to be safe!

2:30. I visited Rachel. Stubborn with a capital S! She won't talk to anyone until she gets out. I told her that then that will be a long time! She refused to eat. She says she is going to hurt herself until she gets out. She didn't want to hear any positive talk. Rachel said it was because she gave in so easily that bad things must have happened to her, so she wasn't going to give in! I kind of like that strength, even though it shouldn't be applied toward people who can help. We talked about my phone call with Luke,

Abigail, and Ben. She likes to hear that stuff. She almost smiled when I talked about our dog, Sophie.

The second morning that I was in the fishbowl, while being walked to the shower, I saw that Lindsay was in the fishbowl room next to mine. When I got back to my room, I moved the tiny mattress to the other wall so that I was against the wall by Lindsay's room. During the night, I began tapping on the wall. Lindsay responded with several taps. I tapped some more, and we began to communicate with taps. The night nurse (who was older and hard to distinguish between a man and a woman and who never smiled) tapped on the Plexiglas and told me to go to sleep and to stop tapping on the wall. I ignored her and kept tapping messages to Lindsay. The nurse slid open the Plexiglas window and insisted that I stop. When she left, I continued with the tapping. She came back with another nurse and security guards. I resisted, but they restrained me and put me into a new isolation room.

If I thought the fishbowl was bad, this new room was horrible! I will forever remember it as being "the dungeon." It was a tiny rust colored brick-lined room with the same thin mattress as before, but there was no pillow or sheet since they thought I might harm myself with such things. I was told to take off my clothes and put on a thin hospital gown. (I couldn't believe that they actually gave me privacy while changing!) There were no windows, and the solid dark brown metal door had a tiny metal slit through which they would pass me my tray of food. I felt like they were terrified to touch me and that I was some crazy rabid animal or a criminal on death row. Yes, I agree that I kind of went psychotic when they removed me from the fishbowl, but I don't think it's right to treat any human being like this.

Anyway, being in that room and being treated like that, I kind of went insane. I tried yelling and screaming, but no one came. I ran around the room like a crazy person and banged myself against the walls. I began punching the brick walls and didn't stop until my knuckles broke open and started to bleed. I finally wore myself out and passed out from exhaustion. The next morning was Monday, and my therapist, Dr. Shey, came rushing in to find me huddled in the corner.

Despite the fact that I had never allowed her to shake my hand or even touch my arm or shoulder, she rushed over to me and held me tightly. She had always been so professional and respected my space, but that morning she held on to me and rocked me back and forth as if I was her little daughter. For the first time in my life, I didn't flinch or feel repulsed from the touch of someone outside of my family. Rather, I enjoyed being held and felt safe and protected.

After sitting on the floor and rocking me back and forth for a while, she helped me get up and helped me into the bathroom to wash up. I looked into the mirror and saw that my hair was all tangled, I had bald spots from me pulling handfuls of hair out, and I looked like a wild woman who hadn't seen civilization in many years. My eyes were enlarged and dilated, and they felt like they were bulging and pounding. Dr. Shey helped me wash my face and brush my hair. She gave me a cold washcloth to put over my eyes and on my face and led me to a back room by the kitchen by the nurses' station. I sat down with the washcloth covering my eyes as she washed my hands and bandaged them with gauze. Exhausted, I just sat there quietly. She asked me if I would promise to sit there until she came back. I was too exhausted to even nod, but she knew I would stay put. I could hear her and the night staff arguing about why I was put in that awful room. She came back and reassured me that I would never be put back there again. I was charged for damaging my room, but I was allowed back. No matter how awful I was or how much damage I caused, she kept her word and I never returned to the dungeon. That was how Dr. Shey gained my trust and how she could convince me to be safe while working through difficult memories. (To this day, I feel horrible for causing so much damage to the hospital, for having my parents pay such a large damaged property bill, and for behaving in such a manner.)

Mom's prayer journal: Dear Lord, remove all doubt and fear from me, but when I see so much sadness in Rachel, then I doubt everything we are doing ... I better end this prayer because I'm tempted to ask "why." Let me fix my eyes on you, trust you! *Believe in* YOU. *Oh, Lord, be with Rachel ... Lord, you must not forsake her. Remove the fear that Rachel has.*

Fill her with hope, peace, and joy. Please spare her any more pain. Let her start healing. Let her see Your hand … Lord, help, I feel so alone. I only imagine how Rachel must feel. Lord, give her comfort now! I can't be there to hold her. My arms around her isn't what she needs anyway. Putting my arms around her is just putting a Band-Aid on a huge wound. Lord, give her comfort and let her sleep in peace. Hold her in Your arms tonight. Hold her close to your heart. Let her feel Your presence. Let her close her eyes trusting in You. Give her peaceful sleep. She needs so desperately to sleep! Let her remember that You hold your dear tender lambs when they are hurting. Hold her tonight and let Your lamb start healing. I feel confident that You heard my prayer. Amen.

I liked Trish, my art therapist. At first, I was embarrassed since I couldn't draw very well, but she soon taught me that it didn't matter how well I drew. All that mattered was to use different art media to express my emotions in a safe and healthy manner. Once I understood that I didn't have to actually draw anything but that I could just draw and color while talking through memories, I found it to be beneficial to my healing. I discovered that I would unconsciously color my emotions or draw details that I didn't even understand until later. It felt safer to talk about memories when I could just draw or color since it gave me something to focus on while talking. Trish helped me create a picture to be used as my "safe place" when going through a difficult time. I drew the sand dunes with tall grass by the ocean, with seagulls flying and a gray sky with the sun poking through the clouds. She helped me describe this favorite childhood memory and taught me how to visualize being back there where I was safe. When I was working through difficult memories and about to dissociate, I learned how to stay present by thinking of this memory. To this day, being at the ocean and hiding in the sand dunes is my favorite memory.

I learned to trust and enjoy talking to one of the night nurses whose name was Evan. I had a difficult time sleeping, so I often came out of my room and sat in the chairs in the living room space. Evan would always be out there reading a book and making sure none of the others left their rooms or sneaked into someone else's room. At first, he scared me since he was a guy. However, he soon gained my trust and I began to open up to him and talk to him about memories. From our conversations, he learned that I enjoyed playing sports and that I was more open when I was busy. Eventually, I trusted him enough to shoot hoops in the courtyard with him and talk about memories. I looked forward to our late night chats, and he became my new older brother. Being with him reminded me of being with Luke and how much I enjoyed our late night chats while we played Ping-pong or Pool. However, that all changed once I began to tell about being raped. Luke kept everything inside and never talked about the rapes, the difficulties of having to leave his life behind, and moving to Wyoming … He was emotionally detached.

While working on memories at Esperanza, it felt as if I had an avalanche of confusing memories. I was working on memories of being raped and tortured by Shawn, Sebastian, and Coach Carl when suddenly I was having memories that didn't make any sense. I was having more and more memories of when I was a little girl when I lived in the South. I kept trying to dismiss these new memories, but the more I shoved them down, the more often they took over my thoughts and the more scared I became of them, causing me to dissociate more often. I couldn't believe the memories, for they turned my sense of reality into a lie. I didn't know what to think or believe. I would have memories of being raped or chased by Shawn, when suddenly I would see and feel myself drowning, or watching my mom drive away, or feel all itchy, like bugs were crawling all over me.

I began to have a Q-tip fetish because it felt as if I had a bug in my ear that would tell the monster that I was talking about our secrets. Whenever I had memories of being a child, I would feel as if a bug were crawling around in my ear, and I would almost go crazy to get that sensation out of my ear. I would take a Q-tip and dig and scrape in there, desperately trying to rid my ear of that creepy feeling. No matter how much digging and scraping I would do, I just could *not* get rid of that noise. To this day, I still have a Q-tip fetish and still hear that buzzing when thinking of childhood memories.

Eventually, I did open up and tell Dr. Shey about my childhood memories:

> *"Come on out, Rachel! Come here! Get over here before I beat you with my cane!" Mr. Nelson would say as I tried to run away and hide. I hid behind a big old reclining chair, but his dog found me. I ran and hid in a tiny dark closet. This closet became my only place of security. Mr. Nelson always found me, but sometimes he would just let me stay in there for a long time. The small closet contained some jackets and a broom. I would sit on a box with my knees pulled up tight to my chin and hug my knees as tightly as possible. I would sit there huddled and hidden behind Mrs. Nelson's long brown fur coat. I loved the soft fur on the coat. I would bury my head into the fur and run my hands and arms up and down the coat. With it being so warm in Georgia, I don't know why she had a fur coat. I had never seen a fur coat before, and I thought it was the most beautiful garment ever. I was so lonely, scared, and desperate for comfort that the only thing that brought me some comfort was the soft fur on that coat.*
>
> *Mr. Nelson never beat me with his cane, even though he always threatened to do so. Instead, he laughed as he pulled me out of the closet by my leg. He would throw me across the room so that I landed on the couch. The couch would rock with the force of me thrown onto it, and before I could get up and run, he would be hovering above me and covering my face with a pillow as he pushed my body down into the couch cushion. As the orange pillow was shoved against my face, all I could smell was dirt and cigar smoke. I could taste the dirt and stiff fabric of the pillow as he tried to smother me and make me go limp. Being a Boston terrier, the dog, King, would jump on me and snort with his tongue hanging out and curled up at the end as he panted. It looked as if his eyes were going to pop out of his head. I absolutely loved animals, but I hated King. I could not get away from that dog.*
>
> *Mr. Nelson would carry me to his bedroom as he shuffled down the hallway with his cane. Since I was his dolly, I wasn't allowed to*

walk or move without his help. Everywhere I looked, I saw brown. The room was lined with wood paneling. The bedspread was an old quilt with different shades of brown and orange. There was an old brown sheet covering the one little window above the bed. Sometimes the sheet was tied back to let in some sunlight, but most of the time, it was dark, dreary, and musty. He would sit me down on the bed and tell me to sit there like a good little dolly. I sat there and watched him go to the closet and pull out a frilly pale yellow dress. I had never seen a dress with so many ruffles and so much lace. It was so pretty, and he was so excited to have me wear it. He came back to the bed and pulled me by my ankles until I was sitting at the edge of the bed. Mr. Nelson liked smelling the dress, even though I never smelled anything on it. He would undress me and help me put the dress on. I hated how the lace made me itch. The inside of the dress made my skin itch, and I would wiggle to relieve the itch. He would slam me down to the bed, shake me several times, yell at me, and pin me to the bed with his cane against my throat. Sometimes the cane pushed me down so much that it was difficult to breathe. It hurt when I swallowed. I hated being pinned down and seeing how angry I had made him. I would look up into his red angry face in terror, and all I saw was an evil monster.

After dressing me in the yellow dress, he would take pictures of me. I hated having my picture taken. He would tell me to smile, but I was so terrified that I just couldn't. He was always so serious when taking pictures of me. He would have me sit on the bed and fluff out the dress so that the ruffles would all lie nicely on the bed beside me. He would reposition my hair so that it hung just so. He would back away from the bed, look in his camera, fix something that wasn't perfect about me, and then back away again and take more pictures.

Sometimes Mr. Nelson's friend came over. His friend was a tall, skinny brown-haired man about the same age as my dad. His left eye was brown, and his right eye was pale blue. He had long brown hair, often had no shirt on, and wore tight blue jeans with big holes in them. Mr. Nelson and his friend would sit in the dark little kitchen drinking beer. I was their little "toy" when they drank. I had to get them their beer bottles from the refrigerator. When I handed them their beer, they would pick me up and have me sit on their laps. They would laugh at me and poke at me and taunt me since I didn't talk or fight back. I just sat there like a dolly. However, I learned to move quickly and carefully when retrieving their beer since I had to dodge the bottles they threw at me. Even though I knew it was coming, the sound of breaking glass always startled me. Between cleaning up the broken glass and retrieving their beer, I was made to sit under the table and sometimes under the chair. Even though I hated being forced to sit under there like the dog, at least I was out of harm's way and I could pretend I was somewhere else far, far away. At first, the sound of the birds chirping outside cheered me and gave me something to think about, but then I got angry at them. I was jealous of the birds I could hear outside. I wished I could sing and fly far away.

I was so lonely and scared that I created "friends" to help me survive. Molly was my friend who protected me. When I was with Molly, I could escape the reality of being with Mr. Nelson, my monster. Molly was smart and always knew what to do to not get Mr. Nelson too angry. Molly always knew how to get locked in the closet in order to escape the monster. When in that closet, I could tell Molly all my fears and cry. When I was Dolly, I could never make a sound, but Molly knew my pain. She knew what I was saying. She could hear my silent crying and see my invisible tears. Molly became my mom when Mom wasn't around.

One day Mr. Nelson's friend "One Blue Eye" brought a little boy named Tommy with him. Tommy was about my age, maybe a little older. He had dirty blond hair that was filthy and clumped together, and he had green eyes. He wore blue pants that were ripped and way too small for him. He had on a red T-shirt that was torn and stained, and his arms, legs, and hands were covered in dirt, bruises, and cuts. I was so excited to have a friend to play with. This was one of the only days I was allowed to stay dressed all day long, and I was even allowed to play outside with Tommy.

I didn't talk to him, and he didn't talk to me, but we were instant friends. We were able to communicate and understand each other without even speaking. We played tag and ran around outside. We sat in Mrs. Nelson's flower garden and hid from King, Mr. Nelson, and One Blue Eye. We dug in the dirt together. He would look at me with those big green eyes as though asking me a silent question and wishing for me to respond. Every noise made him run for cover in Mrs. Nelson's flower garden. He was shy and scared. I remember this being an enjoyable day at Mr. Nelson's house.

Tommy was soon brought back to Mr. Nelson's house. But this day was different. Before Tommy came, I was dressed in the same yellow dress. Tommy came dressed in new clothes and was clean. We were immediately taken to Mr. Nelson's bedroom and photographed together. They undressed us and continued taking more pictures. I don't know what happened or what we did wrong, but suddenly Mr. Nelson and his friend stopped taking pictures of us and became furious. They said we were dirty, pieces of garbage, and so naughty that our parents wouldn't want us anymore. One Blue Eye picked both of us up and carried us outside. He threw us into the garbage/compost pile. He said we were a pile of trash and that we needed to stay there since we were just garbage. "No one will ever love you. You're just garbage. Your parents called us and told us to throw you away. They don't want you anymore. You're so naughty!"

I felt so ashamed. I felt so confused. I felt it was all my fault. I believed them that my parents didn't want me anymore. I believed him that I was dirty and just a piece of trash. The more he yelled at us, the more ashamed I became for being naked next to Tommy. I tried to cover up with the garbage, but it was no use. I felt as if Tommy and everyone else could see right through the little covering I did manage to find and see how dirty I was. The dry grass and little twigs kept poking me. The smell of the rotting plants and garbage was nauseating. The pile was covered in ants, flies, and other bugs that crawled all over me and swarmed my body. My body was soon engulfed with little red fire ants. If you have ever seen fire ants, you know how quickly they can overtake your body and do some pretty serious harm! I lay there whimpering as the ants feasted on my body. Mr. Nelson quickly grabbed me and carried me into the house. He dropped me in the bathtub and filled it with cold water. The cold water soothed my bitten body, but I still ached. I was allowed to get dressed in my normal clothes and didn't see Tommy or One Blue Eye leave. I was told to go sit in the closet until my mom came to pick me up.

The next time I saw Tommy, I was too embarrassed to look at him and he was too embarrassed to look at me. We were able to keep our clothes on, but it was still awkward. Eventually, we began to play together. We spent most of the time hiding in the flower garden, lying with our backs against the ground and looking up at the flowers above us and watching the clouds float by. I liked to watch the tall flowers sway in the breeze; lying in the flower garden with Tommy was so peaceful.

As soon as we heard the screen door slam and heard footsteps on the porch, Tommy quickly put his hand over my mouth and held me down to the ground. He looked so scared yet so determined. We could hear King snorting and panting as he came closer to us and finally found us. As soon as King poked his head between the flowers and was about to jump on us, Tommy quickly grabbed the dog's mouth and held onto the dog's bottom jaw. King started to paw at Tommy's hands and was wiggling around, trying to get away, but Tommy held on tightly and didn't let go.

As King and Tommy were wrestling, Mr. Nelson and his friend came walking over to us. Mr. Nelson grabbed King as One Blue Eye grabbed Tommy. Tommy said his only word to me: "Run!" I saw the panic in his eyes and decided to do as he said. I ran for the back of the house. I was running as fast I could, but King soon jumped on me and tackled me to the ground. I could hear Mr. Nelson's friend yelling and beating Tommy.

Mr. Nelson carried me back into the house and locked me in the closet. I don't know how long I was in there, but it seemed like a pretty long time. When I was finally let out, I saw One Blue Eye *and Tommy sitting on the couch. Tommy was holding a rag to his nose and avoiding looking at me. I was sad that he didn't want to look at me. He was my only friend, and I didn't understand why he didn't want to look at me.*

Tommy and I were picked up and thrown into the back of One Blue Eye's old white pickup truck. We were covered with old burlap bags and told to stay lying down. We were told that if we poked our heads up, we would be clobbered over the head with a board. I don't know about Tommy, but I was too scared to test them. Even though it was a bumpy ride and I was hot, I stayed under that itchy burlap for the entire ride.

When the truck finally stopped and we were told to get up, I saw that we were at a small farm. I saw an old barn, some fenced-in areas, and animals everywhere I looked. I saw some horses, sheep, goats, geese, chickens, and cats. I looked at Tommy and smiled on the inside. I loved animals, and I thought this was a great place to be! Tommy looked terrified and wouldn't look at me. I was allowed to go and look at all the animals. I tried to get Tommy to be happy, but he just kept looking terrified and angry. He wouldn't look at me, yet he wouldn't let me out of his sight. Mr. Nelson and his friend were in the barn, and they called me over to them. As I started to run to the barn, Tommy grabbed my hand and began pulling me the other way. I jerked my hand free and headed to the barn. I went into the barn and saw that they had several baby goats in a barn stall. They opened the stall door and had me come in. They told me I could choose any baby goat to take care of. They even said that I could take it home with me! I thought I was dreaming.

All the baby goats were so cute. I wanted all of them! It was so hard to choose, but I chose a little black goat. They said I could take it outside and play with it. For a while, it stayed close to Tommy and me, and it kept head butting us. I thought it was funny and cute. I loved my new goat. But then it started to wander off. I ran after it to catch it, but the more I ran, the faster and farther away it ran. I was chasing it up a hill when all of a sudden, it dropped out of my sight. I ran to where I last saw it and saw that it had fallen into a large hole. It was making so much noise and was struggling to stand up. Tommy took my arm and tried to pull me away, but I didn't want to leave my hurt goat. Tommy pulled harder and started to get angry with me; that's when Mr. Nelson and his friend came over to me. They saw that the goat had fallen and hurt its leg. They got angry with me for not taking care of my goat. They told me that since I didn't take care of it, I would have to kill it. They pulled the goat out of the hole and carried it to the barn.

Mr. Nelson's friend had a knife, and he killed the goat. I was so scared and sad. I loved animals. I could never kill one! I felt so ashamed for not watching and taking better care of my goat.

After they skinned the goat, I was told I was to be punished. I was carried over to the edge of a deep hole. They pulled on a rope that was attached to a small wooden box. I was undressed and told to lie down in it. It was so small that I had to lie in a fetal position, hugging my knees. They kept telling me what a bad girl I was, how I sinned, how stupid and worthless I was, how I caused the goat to be killed, and now I needed to die. They put a straw-type thing in a little hole on the side of the box. They put it in my mouth and told me to keep it in my mouth. They told me to suck in air and blow it out. Then they closed the lid on the box. It was dark in there. It was hot, and I couldn't move. I felt as if I couldn't breathe. I felt the coffin with me in it being lowered down into the hole. The coffin slightly swung from side to side, sometimes making a sudden drop, while other times being let down slowly. Finally, it rested at the bottom of the hole. The dark and sudden drops made me sick, and I threw up. I was lying on my side and my face was in the vomit, while some of it ran down my side. I tried to keep the straw in my mouth, but it fell out. I couldn't move my arms to put it back in. I tried to find it with my tongue, but it was no use. I started to hear thumps on the cover of the box. I could hear them yelling at me. Every once in a while, little pieces of dirt fell into the little hole on the side of the box. I kept hearing thumps, and sometimes the box bumped, shoving my face back into the vomit. Eventually, the thumps became quiet ...

I don't know if I fell asleep or passed out, but the next thing I knew, the lid of my coffin was removed and the sunlight was streaming in, blinding me. I couldn't see because of the sudden light, and I was so scared I didn't know what was happening. I could hear them talking to me, but I couldn't understand them. Suddenly, I felt a cold gush of water hit my face. Being sprayed in the face stunned and surprised me at first. They said that if I wanted to live, I had to be a good girl and obey them. I was told I couldn't cry or tell anyone about "our little secret." They said that I had to leave my parents since I was so naughty. They kept telling me this repeatedly until I lay there quietly, not moving my face away from the hose water. As soon as I was still, they stopped spraying me with the hose and took me out of the box. I couldn't stand, and I fell to the ground. Mr. Nelson picked me up and took me into his friend's house to wash up.

I didn't see Tommy that day after the box incident. Looking back, I'm sure that he was trying to warn me and protect me. I'm guessing that he experienced a similar incident. I don't know who was a bigger monster—Mr. Nelson or his friend. I can only imagine the horrors that Tommy endured at that farm in the hands of One Blue Eye.

During a different visit to the farm, One Blue Eye came out of the barn swearing and yelling. He was all sweaty and out of breath. He grabbed me and threw me into the back of his truck. He told me to stay under the burlap bags. Mr. Nelson came out of the house and climbed into the truck. We drove a little way over many bumps. I had to hold on tightly to the burlap bag to stay hidden under it. I was told to stay covered up, and I was terrified of them seeing me uncovered. We came to a sudden halt, and I bumped into the edge of the truck.

They slammed their truck doors, uncovered me, and half dragged, half carried me out of the back of the truck. I fell to the ground, and they immediately undressed me. They grabbed a dead rabbit out of a wooden box on the back of the truck and skinned it in front of me. Then they put a rag in the rabbit's blood and smeared me with blood since "that's what gators like to eat." They had me follow them to the edge of the swamp. Once we got there, they pulled on a rope that was tied to a nearby tree. They kept pulling on the rope until a tiny wire cage was exposed. They dragged the cage out of the water, and I saw that another shorter rope was attached to it. At the end of this short rope was a large gray cinder block. They opened the top lid of the cage, threw the dead rabbit in, and shoved me into it. The cage was so small that I couldn't move. I was shoved in so that I was lying on my back with my knees tucked up to my chest. My head was pressed up against one end, while my butt and my scrunched-up feet were against the other end. It was so tight that I had to hug myself to make my shoulders fit. Between being extremely itchy from the blood painted on me, being squished into a tiny wire cage with a dead rabbit for a pillow, hearing the constant buzz of bugs swarming me, and being told I was going to be gator bait, I was terrified. These monsters were completely out of their minds!

With me in it, they dragged the cage over to the edge of the swamp. I first heard the splash of the large cinder block hitting the water, and then I felt the jerk of the cage being pushed into the water. It was so cold and black. The water was so dark that I couldn't see what was in it. They kept talking about the alligators and the water snakes that loved to eat "naughty little girls." The cage began to sink. I could hear them talking, but all I could focus on was the black and-green murky swamp water beginning to engulf me. All I could think about was that there were alligators and snakes in the water just waiting to eat me. As the cage sunk deeper and deeper, sheer terror went through my body. I was trapped. I couldn't move. I was about to be alligator and snake food. I was about to drown. All I could see was the dark water about to cover my face; my only way to breathe and stay alive was about to be covered. I wanted to yell, but I was too full of terror. I wanted to cry, but I couldn't even do that. I was able to wiggle enough to reach up and grab the wire above me. I clung to those wire bars with a death grip. I was able to move my feet enough so that I could use my toes to hang on *to the wires. I hung on for dear life and so desperately tried to pull myself up against the lid of the cage. They saw that I was clinging to the wires, so they smashed my fingers and toes with a stick until I let go. They told me to say good-bye since they saw an alligator coming toward me and that I was about to become its lunch. They said that maybe I could pray to Jesus to save me. I tried praying, but nothing happened. They kept saying that the alligator was getting closer and closer and that I need to keep trying to pray.*

Then they took a stick and submerged the wire cage. I believed them that an alligator was about to eat me. I wasn't ready to go under the water, and I began to suck in water. I tried to find the wires to hang on to, but I couldn't breathe. I was trapped inside a tiny cage underwater. I couldn't even thrash around gasping for air since the cage was so tiny. All I could do was watch the dark water cover me. I sunk so quickly that I couldn't even take a breath. My lungs quickly filled up with swamp water. I thought I was going to die. My throat felt as if it were on fire, and my head felt as if it were going to explode. All I could see was the murky black water. I was finally pulled up so that my face was above the water. They said that they were in charge and that only they could save me. They said I was a stupid little girl for praying to Jesus. They said that Jesus didn't save me since I was too stupid, dirty, and naughty. I felt horrible.

I was choking and coughing and shaking. They just laughed at me and poked me with sticks. I stopped coughing, and they submerged me into the water again before I could take a breath. My heart was pounding, I couldn't breathe, and I couldn't move. I was terrified to death. This time, they pulled me all the way up the bank near the tree. I was coughing and choking the whole time as they laughed. They asked if I had learned my lesson, and they opened the lid. I couldn't move. I had no energy left. I was literally scared to death. I was as limp as a wet noodle. They picked me up, and I just slumped over the friend's shoulder as he carried me back to his truck. I learned my lesson all right; I learned that my life was in their evil hands. I learned how evil these monsters were and what it felt like to be so trapped and terrified out of my mind.

Thankfully, my brain was able to segment and I was able to create "friends" to help me cope with such terror. These "friends" were able to hold these horrific memories for me so that I could stay sane and continue to function as a regular child.

Mr. Nelson would often tell me that my family wanted to get rid of me and that they didn't love me anymore. He kept telling me that I was nothing but garbage. He told me that he was going to find me a new family since I wasn't loved anymore. I believed him. I believed him that my own family didn't love me anymore. I believed him that I caused my dad to be angry. I believed him that it was my fault that Dad wasn't with us anymore. I believed him that my dad left since I was so naughty. I believed him that I saw my mom crying because she hated me so much. I was so trusting and naive that I believed all of Mr. Nelson's lies.

Mr. Nelson began taking me for car rides to meet my "new family." We went in his old brown car. He would have me lie down on the floor in the back seat. I rested my head on the floor hump, and he covered me up with a scratchy maroon blanket. He would tell me to stay under the blanket and then gently cover my face with a rag and tell me to go to sleep. The hum of the road under the car tires was soothing, and I would quickly fall asleep. I would only wake up when he would go over some huge bumps and then suddenly stop the car. I had to stay under the blanket until he lifted it off me and told me to come out.

He would carry me to the side of a big white house with a large porch. There was a large grassy area and trees all around the house. On the side of the house was a slanted door covering a root cellar. He would push me down a few steps into a dark, low room. The room was small with a dirt floor, and the ceiling was so low that Mr. Nelson had to bend over while in the room, which was lined with wire dog crates. There were three cages lined up next to each other on each side of the room and they were two crates high. Inside each crate was a naked young child. They all looked so forlorn, dirty, and lifeless. It was so quiet in there that it was eerie. My clothes were removed and I was put into the top cage in the middle of the row. I had nothing to sit on except the hard wire bars. Mr. Nelson locked the crate and told me to be quiet. He went up the steps, and the door slammed shut. It was so dark that I couldn't see anything. The air was cool, but the smell of feces and urine wafted in the air. No one made a noise. All was quiet except for the occasional sound of someone changing position in a cage. As much as I tried, I couldn't get comfortable. My bottom hurt from sitting on the wire floor of my cage. I tried to curl up and lie down and try to hide from the child below me, but there wasn't enough room to move around.

During one of these visits, I don't know if I fell asleep or just lost track of time, but suddenly sunlight streamed into the little dungeon room and I heard One Blue Eye telling Tommy to behave. It took a while for my eyes to adjust to the light, but then I saw that Tommy was put into the last top cage adjacent to mine. One Blue Eye quickly left, and the door slammed shut. We were left in darkness again. Now all the cages were full. It was too dark to see Tommy's face, but I put my hand up to the cage wall, and he must have done the same thing, for our fingers touched. We sat there holding on to each other's fingers. I don't know if I held on to him to comfort him or to comfort myself, but it was nice to know that I had a friend and that I wasn't all alone in this dungeon.

A little while later, a man opened the door and came down the steps. He opened the first bottom cage across from me and reached in to pull out a dark-haired little girl about my age. She huddled as far back as she could, and the man struggled to reach her. He took hold of her ankle and pulled her out as she started crying and grabbing at anything she could reach to grasp. The man got angry and slammed her to the ground several times. She finally stopped fighting and crying, and he dragged her limp body by her ankles to the steps and then carried her limp body up the steps. The whole *time this was happening, Tommy held on to my fingers tighter and squeezed them.*

Hearing and seeing how terrified she was to go with that man frightened me. I didn't know who he was, what was going to happen to me, or where we were. Tommy must have known what was going to happen to her since he held on tighter and began to tremble. I was scared and quietly began to sing "Jesus Loves Me" since that was what my mom would always sing to me. I don't know if anyone heard me, but Tommy stopped trembling and squeezed my hand. I quietly sang it several times, and then the door opened and light streamed in, making it difficult to see. I couldn't see, but I could smell him. Mr. Nelson had come for me.

He was bent over and unlocking my cage. He pulled me out, and I dropped to the dirt floor. Mr. Nelson shoved me toward the steps. As I crawled over to the steps, I could hear Tommy sniffling. I turned around and saw Tommy crying and shaking the door of his cage. Mr. Nelson got mad and yelled at him to stop making so much noise. Tommy kept crying and shaking the cage door as Mr. Nelson pushed me up the steps. My feet and legs must have fallen asleep while I was in the cage, since I fell to the ground once we were outside. Mr. Nelson carried me around the house to the front porch, and we went inside.

The house was a beautiful mansion. We entered a large open room that had a huge rug, several fancy chairs, and a beautiful stairway that went to a balcony that wrapped around the perimeter of the second floor. I had never seen such a beautiful place before. It was so clean and elegant, and everything was so large. As soon as we entered the room, a woman with curly black, white, and gray hair quickly came down the steps, grabbed my hand, and marched me upstairs to a large white bathroom. She quickly put me into a white alligator claw bathtub that was filled with steaming hot water and full of bubbles. As much as I enjoy bubble baths, I couldn't enjoy this bath. She was scrubbing me so hard with a brush that I thought she would rub me raw. I don't know if my body turned red from the scalding hot water, from the intense scrubbing, or from both, but by the end of the bath, my body was numb. When she washed my hair, she dunked my head under the water and held it down. This wasn't how my mom washed me, and I was scared and confused. She picked me out of the bathtub and had me sit on the black-and-white tiled floor while she dried my hair. I sat on the floor looking at the alligator claws of the bathtub, wondering if I was going to be alligator bait again. She dried my hair, brushed it, and put a ribbon in my hair. She got mad since the ribbon kept falling out of my hair and she couldn't get my hair to stay where she wanted it. She finally gave up with the ribbon, brushed my hair again, and dressed me in Mr. Nelson's pale yellow dress.

As she took my hand and led me down the stairs, she told me to be a good dolly and to do whatever my new family told me to do. We walked over to one of the many large doors in the huge entrance. She knocked on the door and opened it at the same time. She gently shoved me into a dim office. She walked over to the dark wooden desk and sat down in a chair behind it. I just stood there frozen, not knowing what to do. She got up from the chair and guided me into the room, but she didn't give me any orders or hints of how she wanted me to behave. Across from the desk sat a nice-looking couple on a red couch. They smiled at me, and I was instantly shy and looked down at the rug-covered floor. They looked like a nice friendly couple, but I didn't want a new family. I wanted my mom, dad, and brother. The woman who bathed me introduced me to them, saying my name was Raelyn, and then told me to go over and meet my new family. The woman who was "my new mom" got off the couch and came toward me. Before she could get too close to me, I turned around and bolted for the door. I was just running out the door when I ran into Mr. Nelson, who was coming into the room holding some papers. When I bumped into Mr. Nelson, he dropped his papers and I saw pictures of me wearing the same yellow dress spill onto the floor. He quickly grabbed me and held me tightly, whispering in my ear that if I didn't behave, I'd become gator food. He took my hand and led me back into the room with the couple.

As Mr. Nelson led me over to the couple, I could see that the wife was crying and the husband was holding her hand. Mr. Nelson and the lady who bathed me apologized for my running away like that and reassured them that I wouldn't do that again. They took me outside to the front porch, and I sat with the nice couple on the porch swing. I looked at the woman with curly blonde hair and her tall blond husband and thought they were nice, but the more they talked and asked me questions, the more I missed my real family. They asked me many questions, but I didn't answer. I didn't say a single word. They kept calling me Raelyn, which really confused me. I didn't know how this Raelyn girl was supposed to act or what she was supposed to do, so I just sat there quietly looking at my brown buckled shoes and white lacy socks, thinking about my real mom. The blonde woman started to cry, and they took me back into the office. The couple was sad that I wouldn't talk to them and never even looked at them. They told Mr. Nelson that they didn't want me, and then they left. As soon as they left the office, Mr. Nelson began yelling at me and said that I had ruined everything. We soon left to go back to Mr. Nelson's house.

The next time we went to that big white mansion, it was a much different scenario. I was still taken to the little dungeon, but this time Tommy was already in his cage. Again, Tommy and I clung to each other's fingers through the wire walls of our prison as I sang "Jesus Loves Me." Mr. Nelson came for me, dragged me out of the cage, and took me inside the house. The same woman with striped hair came down the stairs to get me again. She went through the same washing routine of scrubbing me raw and clean. However, this time she dressed me in a white summer dress, white lacy socks, and shiny black dress shoes. She took me down the stairs, and Mr. Nelson met me at the bottom of the stairs and led me to a different large door. At the door, Mr. Nelson firmly told me to be a good dolly and do what the man told me to do. He opened the door and led me into a room that was lined with floor-to-ceiling bookshelves. There were several fancy chairs, a huge fireplace, and a fancy red couch. On that couch was an older man who was about *the same age at Mr. Nelson. He was a red-faced bald fat man who was sweating and continuing to push his glasses back in place. When he wasn't adjusting his glasses, he was clenching his hands together and rubbing them back and forth. Mr. Nelson was sitting in a chair across from him and had me sit on his lap while talking to this man. Finally, Mr. Nelson stood up and put me down, telling me to make his friend happy by being a good little dolly.*

With that, Mr. Nelson walked out the door and shut the door. The fat man told me to come over by him, so I did, sitting down on the couch next to him. He instantly began to touch my hair, smell it, and play with it. The more he played with my hair, the more he would sweat, and his glasses kept slipping down his nose. Mr. Nelson soon returned, sat down in the same chair as before, and had me come over and sit in his lap again. As I sat there, he asked the fat man how he enjoyed his visit. He replied that he enjoyed it very much and would like another visit very soon. They shook hands and then we went back to Mr. Nelson's house.

The next visit, I was dressed in the same white dress, white socks, and black shoes, and I visited with "Fat Guy" again. He had me sit in his lap, and he began to touch me. His red fat face was dripping with sweat, and his glasses kept slipping down, so he finally had to take them off and place them on the couch next to him. He continued to molest me until there was a knock at the door and Mr. Nelson quickly came into the room. Fat Guy quickly stopped and told Mr. Nelson that he wanted some more time with me, but Mr. Nelson said that his time was up. Mr. Nelson picked me up and took me to the lady who bathed me. She took me upstairs to the bathroom, and once we were there, she began yelling at me. "How could you do that? You're such a dirty girl! What a naughty little girl!" She scrubbed my face, arms, and hands with a nailbrush and soap. She put me back into my normal clothes and led me outside to Mr. Nelson, who was waiting by his car.

I was confused and didn't understand why she was angry at me. I did what they told me to do—I was the good little dolly who did exactly what Fat Guy wanted me to do. Mr. Nelson put me on the floor in the back seat of his car and covered me up. He told me that I would soon go and live with my new daddy. He told me I was a good little dolly and made him very happy. Now I was even more confused. She told me I was a dirty, naughty little girl and he was telling me that I was good and making him happy. Which was it? Besides being confused, I was sad and lonely. I didn't want a new daddy. I just wanted my dad back.

The next day, Mr. Nelson had me sit on his big bed while he stuffed a large black garbage bag full of clothes. He quickly took clothes out of his closet and dresser while mumbling to himself and shoving the clothes into the bag. He tied it closed, turned to me, and said, "Are you ready to meet your new daddy, Raelyn?" I just sat there and looked at him. I didn't comprehend why he said my new name was Raelyn. I thought it was a pretty name, but I didn't understand why he had me practice saying it over and over again. I couldn't say it correctly. Instead of saying Raelyn it sounded like "Waywin." He picked me up and put me on the floor of his old brown car. Once again, he covered me up with the blanket and told me to go to sleep.

As soon as he closed the car door, I knew something was different. I heard another car drive into the driveway, and I heard Mr. Nelson yelling. I didn't know who he was yelling at, but he quickly got into the driver's seat and sped away. He was swearing and yelling while he was driving. He was swerving back and forth, so I kept hitting my head against the door and back seat and the blanket slid off me. This time I did not fall asleep but rather wondered what was going on. Mr. Nelson soon pulled over onto the side of the road as another car stopped right next to Mr. Nelson. I was still lying down on the floor, but I could hear Mr. Nelson yelling at Mrs. Nelson. She kept yelling to let me go and said that "she" is starting to ask questions and that it's not safe. I didn't understand what Mrs. Nelson was talking about. Who was "she"? What wasn't safe? Why wasn't it safe? Was I in more danger? Why were they yelling so much? Did I do something wrong to make them so angry? What was going on? What was going to happen?

Suddenly, the car door was yanked open and I was grabbed. Mrs. Nelson was pulling on my arm to get me out of the car, but Mr. Nelson kept yelling at her and got back into the car. Mr. Nelson gunned the engine and began to drive off. Mrs. Nelson was able to drag me out of the car just as he sped off. The back door that I was just dragged out of was flopping back and forth as he drove off. Mrs. Nelson and I sat alongside the road for a little while. What just happened? Where was Mr. Nelson going? What were Mrs. Nelson and I going to do? Where was she going to take me? The fear of the unknown was scarier than knowing we were on our way to the white house full of monsters. I didn't know how she wanted me to behave. Even though Mr. Nelson was an evil monster, I wanted him back. At least I knew what to expect when I was around him.

Mrs. Nelson had me sit in the front seat of her car. I stared out the window and watched as we drove past a horse farm, several small houses, and lots of tall trees. We pulled back into the Nelsons' driveway, and when we approached the house, I saw King standing on the porch looking at us. Mrs. Nelson told me to stay in the car until she came out to get me. She went in the house and locked King in the bedroom. Then she came back to let me out of the car. She had me go to the kitchen to eat a snack of raisins, water, and crackers. She asked me if I was okay. She was being nice to me, but I didn't trust her and didn't say anything. I was hungry, so I quietly ate my snack. When I finished eating, she went outside to water her flowers. I sat there for a while all by myself, but then I quietly snuck over to the door and watched her. I didn't know if I could trust her or not, but I was curious and oddly felt safe around her. When she went around the corner, I went out to the porch so I could see her. She turned around and saw me on the porch. She gently asked me if I wanted to help her. I went over to her, and she had me help her pick flowers for a vase.

That was my last day at the Nelsons' house. My "friends" Dolly, Molly, and Waywin knew I couldn't handle all these horrific experiences, so they took over and held on to all those memories. They kept all those memories locked in a faraway box in my unconscious mind. I was left not remembering or knowing that anything awful had happened at the Nelsons' house.

Soon after my last day with the Nelson's, life returned to "normal." My dad was back at home with us, and my sister Abigail was born. My dad resigned from the ministry, and we soon packed up and moved back to Wyoming to be with family and friends. Several months later, my dad returned to the ministry and received a call to preach on the West Coast.

When I'm asked about Mr. Nelson, I don't even know how to describe him or the trauma I endured while in his care. How could I even fathom this degree of evilness? Yes, he molested me, but it's the sheer terror that's so hard to explain. He never hit me or left any visible marks on me for my mom to notice. Rather, he left deep gaping ravines in my soul that will leave a mark for the rest of my life. I can choose to wallow in self-pity and live my life in bitterness or I can choose to embrace my new self and live my life in peace through the grace of Jesus Christ. With Christ's help, I am more than a conqueror.

Thankfully, while I was at Esperanza Psychiatric Hospital, I learned many useful relaxation and calming methods to keep me present during the day. I learned how to look at these memories and cope with them in a healthy manner. I was finally discharged in July.

Abigail: Dad had stayed in Dallas with you while Mom came to Wyoming for a little while. I was excited to drive to Texas and visit you because we got to take Aunt Gina's brand new Nissan Altima car. It was the nicest car I had ever been in, and Ben and I got the entire back seat to ourselves! We had never traveled in such luxury! I remember Mom warning me that you were a little different than the last time I saw you. She told us about some scars and cuts on your arms and how things were at the hospital. We were sitting in the front lobby area, and this girl who was a patient was sitting there on a couch. She had dyed black hair, was dressed all in black, and had dark goth makeup on. I remember thinking, But my sister isn't a freak like her! *Luke, Ben, and I were sitting in that front lobby waiting to see you since there had just been an issue with your seeing orange juice and having a flashback or dissociative moment.*

Seeing you in Dallas was strange … You were not my sister. It's hard to explain, but I felt I had no idea who you were or how to talk to you. We were prepped on all the triggers we had to avoid: orange juice, roses, Mickey Mouse, bells, and so forth. The most memorable moment from Dallas was seeing Dad cry for the first time in my life. You were playing the song "Hero" by Mariah Carey on the piano, and I was singing along—and Dad cried.

Chapter 21

When I was discharged from Esperanza, I joined my family, who lived in Wyoming. We lived in a blue ranch-style house close to where my grandparents and relatives lived. My mom worked for my uncle at his stock brokerage firm, and my dad worked at the factory and gas station, also filling in for pastors who were on vacation. Luke was enrolled as a senior at the nearby Christian high school and was busy at his photo company job. Abigail was enrolled in fifth grade at a nearby Christian school, and Ben was in first grade at the same school as Abigail.

Abigail: Most of my memories from this whole ordeal are from when we were all together again in Wyoming. I mothered Ben a lot, I helped with meal prep, and I looked forward to when you were "RayRay" because you'd play with me as if you were younger. When knives went missing, we all searched your room; I was proud of myself for finding knives and a belt hidden inside one of your stuffed animals. It was kind of like an Easter egg hunt. I knew how to take Ben in another room and play with him when you had dissociative episodes. I never remember it being a big deal. This was all just normal everyday life in our house. There were times I was scared, sad, and angry. Mom and Dad still parented us, we still did things as a family, and I still sang in a children's choir, still went to camps, and did other activities. Life just went on.

However, I definitely struggled emotionally in my teenage years. I think most of that was just normal teenage girl hormones and drama, not necessarily tied to what happened to Rachel. But I remember days just absolutely hating school and feeling like such an outsider. I hated listening to the other girls complain about their "hard lives" and their shallow problems. I always felt like, "Are you kidding me? You have no idea what my family has been through!" So many times I just wanted to get in front of class and share your story, but I knew it wouldn't serve any purpose at that time. Once in high school, on a particularly bad day, I was staying home from school and having a "mental health day," as we called it. I broke down crying and told Mom that I was feeling guilty because I wished you had died because it all took up so much of Mom and Dad's time. I was jealous, as crazy as that sounds. In my teenage angst, I almost wished something bad would happen to me so I could become a bigger priority to Mom and Dad. I was very dramatic with my emotions, crying and slamming many doors. I feel embarrassed about that now as an adult. But honestly, those years at ages ten, eleven, twelve, and thirteen, I never felt like that. I think it was just normal teenage girl emotions and my wanting attention that caused me to act the way I did in high school.

Dad: It was about the time we moved to Wyoming, and a little after, that we got in touch with a private detective (who was a retired cop) and did some digging. I don't remember how we got in touch with him or even if we had to pay him anything. We never met face-to-face. What I do remember about him was that he found some things that he thought we'd be better off not knowing. What he meant by that, I guess we'll never know. By the time we heard from him, we had moved into the blue house. I was scrambling to find a job, and we were trying to find a therapist for you that could be trusted. A part of that time in the story of our lives was trying to pay bills—think of the costs of therapy, hospitalization bills, and trying to keep up our own health insurance and so forth. The call to teach at the high school was more of a gift from God than you might think! More than just a job, it was health insurance we needed and would not have been able to get for what would have been a "preexisting condition."

To help me transition from Esperanza, an intense inpatient hospital environment, to the "real world," I was admitted to an outpatient program at Jefferson Memorial Hospital. I would go here for half a day for therapy five days a week.

I hated having to start all over and re-explain why I was in need of therapy. Most of the teens on my unit there had eating disorders or drug issues, so I felt I had nothing in common with them. I could be dismissed as soon as my parents found me a counselor to help me with my issues. My mom made an appointment for me to see Dr. Bailey, so I was dismissed after only two weeks!

Mom and I drove up to Dr. Bailey's office building. A multistory glass building, it had elaborate landscaping and appeared to be extremely professional and modern. We went up the elevator to her office and entered a cold and modern waiting room. I went into her office, which had several abstract paintings on the wall and had very uncomfortable furniture. One wall of her office was all glass windows that overlooked beautiful birch trees and a wooded area. I immediately disliked Dr. Bailey. She was too professional, impersonal, and impatient. I didn't trust her at all, so I just stared out the windows. I was thankful that the scenery was so beautiful, for everything else about her was disgusting.

We came back the next week, and this time Dr. Bailey had my mom come in with me since I refused to talk to her. Mom explained the situation to her, and Dr. Bailey told her to have me watch the movie *Schindler's List* to help get memories out. That was the straw that broke the camel's back … Mom and I looked at each other, got up, and left. We never returned. We were stunned that she would want me to watch such a violent and gruesome movie when I myself was so sensitive and quick to dissociate from the mere idea of violence. To this day, we still joke about Dr. Bailey and how she would've made me even crazier!

Since I still didn't have a regular counselor, it was recommended that I join the Survivors of Sexual Assault Support Group at Jefferson Memorial Hospital. I went to the support group once a week and really enjoyed being a part of this group. At first, it really scared me and brought back many memories since I heard other people share their experiences. However, at the same time, it was reassuring, empowering, and motivational for me. As horrible as it sounds, it was reassuring to know that I wasn't the only one who was raped or abused as a child. I wasn't alone with my pain. There were others out there who understood my pain and what I was going through! I had a group of people who knew and understood my issues. They were there to support me through difficult times, and they understood my sense of humor about such things. They made me feel as if I was a person again … not just a messed up girl who was raped. They made me feel worthy of living a life and fulfilling my dreams. The teens who were further along in their therapy were able to motivate me and help me realize that it would get better and that I could still have a great life and have reasons to laugh. As difficult as these meetings were, I looked forward to them.

One stormy summer evening, Mom and I drove to the hospital for group. On the way there, I was troubled, working through some difficult memories, and I had a difficult time staying present. During group that night, some group members were discussing childhood memories and how those memories (good or bad) affected their lives. This topic struck a raw nerve with me and sparked an uncontrollable avalanche of childhood memories. I soon switched between Dolly, Waywin, and Vaca. Dolly and Waywin were young personalities who were extremely terrified. Vaca was aggressive, powerful, and at times seemed demonic. Vaca's "job" was to protect me from any harm. Vaca was successful in this by being so violent and scaring people away from me. I (Vaca) once became so violent and disturbed in group that the group leader had to call hospital security guards. As the three tall and muscular security guards in dark blue-black uniforms with guns at their hips were trying to restrain me I completely lost it and became extremely violent. I struck out at them and kicked at them, fighting for my life. I charged them and wanted to hurt them before they hurt me. The group leader called my mom and called for more backup. When the backup arrived, they overpowered me and put me on a gurney with leather restraints for my legs and arms. Being restrained and held down against my will freaked me out, and I continued to struggle. I fought so hard that I got free from the two leather straps restraining my arms. Before I could do any more damage, hurt myself, or hurt others, the hospital staff injected a syringe of medicine into my thigh. I went limp and fell asleep. I was admitted to the hospital overnight.

The next morning, I woke up not knowing where I was. I was once again restrained to a hospital bed. I began to panic in my confusion. Thankfully, Mom quickly saw that I was awake and came over to my bed. Mom explained that I was at the hospital and that I was restrained so that I wouldn't hurt myself or the nurses. She explained that I had a difficult time in group and that I had dissociated. Mom buzzed for the nurse, and when the nurse came in, she removed my restraints. I had no memory of the security guards or that I had dissociated. Once the restraints were removed, I was calm and wholly Rachel.

In August, I started my sophomore year of high school. Keep in mind that I had dropped out of school early spring of my freshman year, that most of my trauma happened on school property, and that I had just spent part of spring and the entire summer at psychiatric hospitals undergoing intense therapy. Let's just say that my focus at school was *not* on academics! Yes, it was helpful knowing that Luke, my cousins, and my dad were at the same high school and that this was a much safer high school than my previous school, but just the smells and the sounds of a high school triggered so many flashbacks. Not only did I have to worry about being the new kid at the school and trying to fit in, but I also had to deal with constant flashbacks. I was hypervigilant, terrified that I would be trapped in a corner, run into one of my attackers, and terrified that *something* would happen to me.

I remember sitting in science class and staring at the outlet on my desk, planning how to hurt myself. I found myself considering how to "accidentally" burn myself with the Bunsen burner. There were so many sharp tools that would be perfect for hurting myself. Thinking about such things made me almost in a trancelike state. I would think about hurting myself, which reminded me *why* I needed to hurt myself. When I remembered why, I would start thinking about memories. These memories often frightened me so much that I would dissociate and begin to shake. My dad, who was teaching, was often called to come get me out of class. After a few weeks of trying to be "normal" and trying to function, it was soon apparent that it just was not going to work.

Dad: part of my daily teacher prep included a prayer on your behalf, that you'd have a good day, make it through the day without an episode! During this time, there were at least a couple of times when you had a dissociative episode while at school. When it happened, one of the faculty members was instructed to come and fill in for me in my classroom while I'd try to "calm you down." I don't remember being particularly effective at that, and looking back on it now, I'm pretty sure it was a matter of the school trying to be sure that no one would get hurt—either you or a teacher! When you'd dissociate, you often became quite violent. I have several broken ribs to prove it! I also think that most of the teachers were scared of you ... and probably with good reason! I don't remember what the particular "triggers" were at the school, but I do recall that you had a number of them that needed to be avoided.

My parents began the tedious work of fighting for my student rights and getting me the education I needed. Not very many educators knew about my dissociation disorder or how to deal with someone who had such severe PTSD, and my parents had to educate them and explain in detail why a "normal" high school just would not work. After many meetings, assessments, interviews, and lots of hard work done by my parents, the nearby public school district agreed that the area public school could not meet my unique needs. It was agreed upon that I would attend Grantwood Alternative High School and that it would be covered by the public school district.

Grantwood High School is an alternative high school on the grounds of the psychiatric hospital. It is a half-day program with a student-teacher ratio of five to one. Students who attended Grantwood had many issues, including alcoholism, drug abuse, ADHD, anger issues, health issues, and other mental health issues that prevented them from learning in a typical school setting. The staff is well trained in how to teach "troubled" teens and is skilled in handling many different scenarios.

This was the perfect school setting for me since I could go to counseling in the morning and then attend school in the afternoon.

The school itself was in an old building that looked like a house. The schedule was flexible, the class sizes small, and the therapeutic setup of the school helped me focus on my education and forget that I was at a high school. I wasn't constantly triggered by being there. I was able to slowly open up and trust teachers and other kids, make friends, and focus on my learning. The school itself was perfect. I, however, was not the perfect student.

Being new to the school, I wanted to prove to others that I was tough and that nothing would bother me. I felt that I had to prove to others that I was "bad" enough to hang with them. I'm sure they could see right past that mask, but nevertheless, they included me. It was a most interesting group of kids—we all had our own issues, but we all accepted each other for who we were. I quickly became the "counselor" of the group and was sought out to help them with their issues. I still had major trust issues and had to learn that I could trust adults and other kids.

Even though the school setting didn't trigger any memories, I still had flashbacks during class and would often dissociate. Sometimes I would become violent and kick and punch my teachers. Bless their hearts—they never held that against me and continued to pour their hearts out to me and teach me. One of my favorite teachers, Nancy, said that I was the most difficult student she had ever worked with, but that I also had the most promise since I worked so hard at getting better. I will always be thankful to Nancy since she helped me turn my life around.

One day while in speech class, Nancy asked us, "Where do you see yourself in ten years?" I thought she was crazy at first since it was hard enough for me even to think past one day. I just thought that I was a messed-up girl and that I would never finish school and most likely have to live with my parents the rest of my life. Being upset and wanting to prove to her that I was nothing and would never add up to much, I wrote down the most outlandish goals I could think of and then turned them in with a smirk on my face. I expected Nancy to be disappointed and to have me rewrite my goals, but instead she just smiled and walked over to me. Smiling, she stood by me and told me, "Yes, I believe that you will accomplish all these goals. I believe in you, and I know you will be successful." I couldn't believe what I heard! How could she say such things? Just the other day I couldn't sit through class without dissociating and getting violent with her! After a while, my shock and anger at Nancy turned into the belief that maybe, just maybe, she was right. Maybe I was not as messed up as I thought I was.

Nancy's comment and the fact that I knew someone believed in me turned my life around. I stopped being a difficult student and started believing in myself. That was the beginning of when I truly began to live …

The spring of 2006, the principal of Grantwood School called me and asked if I would be willing to speak at the 2006 graduation. Here is the graduation speech I wrote and presented:

Dear Grantwood graduates,

Wow, doesn't that sound nice? Congratulations!

It doesn't seem that long ago when I too was a student at Grantwood. I came to Grantwood in 1994 after dropping out of high school my freshman year. When I dropped out of school, I was told that I most likely would never finish school and that if I did, I probably wouldn't be able to live a "normal" life. So when I began at Grantwood, I had an attitude that I was too broken to be fixed, that I wouldn't amount to anything, and that I was too messed up. I had a very difficult time trusting people, and my self-esteem was quite low. I tried to be tough and act as if I didn't need help. I was upset that my parents enrolled me in school. Looking back, I'm sure I tested the patience of my teachers many times! Over the year, I slowly learned to trust the staff at Grantwood, my attitude began to change, and the staff was slowly chipping away the walls I built around me.

One day while sitting upstairs in Nancy's classroom, she asked me, "Where do you see yourself in ten years?" I don't remember if I laughed aloud or if I just laughed at that idea in my head. I mean, how in the world could I think about where I would be in ten years? I could hardly think past tomorrow, let alone ten years from now! Nancy kept asking me questions and telling me to think big. She told me that if I believed in myself and wanted it bad enough, I would succeed and accomplish my goals. She told me to think big, so still upset about the idea of thinking so far down the road, I decided to come up with the most outlandish goals that I could think of and then prove to her that she was wrong and that I wouldn't be able to accomplish my goals. So I sat there for a while and began to write … Graduate from high school with all As … play on a professional soccer team … graduate from college with all As … marry the most loving, understanding, patient man … get hired for my dream job … maybe have children … be filthy rich …

After writing this down and handing it in with a smirk on my face, prepared to be told to redo it and write more realistic goals, I sat back and watched Nancy read my goals quietly to herself. Well, I didn't get the reaction I was hoping for or expecting. Nancy came over to me smiling and told me, "Yes, if you truly believe that you can do this and if you want it bad enough, you will accomplish all these goals." For the next couple of days, I was determined to prove her wrong. How could she have so much faith in me?

Thankfully, Nancy and all my other teachers were able to see past my attitude. I kept thinking that they must be seeing a different Rachel … all I saw was a messed up gal. All they saw was a girl who overcame many difficulties and who had so much potential. Somehow I slowly began to see what they saw – the Rachel with potential and the determination to succeed. Since I'm so competitive, I took Nancy's assignment as a challenge. I never back down to a challenge, and I certainly won't back down without a fight!

To make the story short, Nancy was right. I have accomplished many of my goals. After being at Grantwood for a year, I went to the area Christian high school my junior and senior year. I graduated from high school in 1997. Unlike my original goals, I didn't graduate with all As but was pretty close with a GPA of 3.67.

I then began college at a nearby university. While at college, I continued playing soccer and played on the university soccer team. It was not quite a professional soccer team, but playing soccer for a *university and winning first place for our conference felt pretty close to playing on a professional team!*

My freshman year in college I met and fell in love with my husband. In October of 2000, we got married. As far as this goal, I went way beyond my dreams—my husband is more loving, patient, and understanding than I could ever have dreamed of.

After getting married, I transferred to a college near the town we lived in and graduated in 2002. Again, not with all As—but close, with a GPA of 3.8. After my very first interview, I was hired to teach second grade. This truly is my dream job, being able to make a difference in children's lives and hopefully motivating them to dream big and achieve their dreams, just as the staff at Grantwood did for me. In 2003, I enrolled in a master's degree program. In July of 2004, my beautiful, happy, energetic son was born. I never knew how much fun and rewarding being a mom would be. He truly is my pride and joy! Having children is my greatest blessing. Last summer I graduated from the university with my master's degree in education—this time I did graduate with all As! My last original goal was to be filthy rich … Well, I'm not filthy rich (actually far from it!), but I'm filthy rich in so many other ways.

I didn't mean to brag about my accomplishments, but I wanted to show you and prove to you that you can and will succeed. Call me a dreamer, but I'm convinced that achieving your full potential is still a goal worth striving for—that excellence is still worth pursuing, even if most people say you can't achieve it. While there may not be many people who strive and live out their dreams despite what others say and think, there are still a few people who do … a very important few. I want each of you to be one of those important few people who strive for their dreams and achieve them. As Nancy said to me, if you believe in yourself and want it bad enough, you will succeed.

Sure, it's not always going to be easy. In fact, I had many bumps and distractions along the way of achieving my goals. My family used to live along the West Coast, where there are many beautiful mountains. When things get challenging, my family likes to compare life to climbing a mountain. When climbing a mountain, there are many uphill battles. When life seems to be very challenging and daunting, it feels as if you're at the bottom of a large and ominous mountain. At times, it can feel hopeless and even impossible. I often felt like surrendering and giving up on achieving my dreams. I have learned that even when it seems impossible to conquer those enormous mountains, there is a way to get to the top of the mountain.

However, you'll need one essential quality: vision. Vision is the ability to see past the obstacles, to focus on your dreams in spite of the obstacles. When you have vision, it affects your attitude. Your attitude is optimistic rather than pessimistic. So when a situation comes that may stop you in your path, you don't throw up your arms and panic. You don't give up. Instead, you say, "This is my moment. This is when I prove to myself how strong I am. I am going to make it to the top of the mountain." There is an important dimension to hanging tough that you dare not miss. It is the thing that keeps you going. I call it a dream. This is nothing more than having a strong belief in the power of having a vision and having confidence in yourself. Refuse to give in to temptation, pessimistic beliefs, and doubts. Belief in yourself is terribly important. Determination is hanging tough when the going gets rough. I'm sorry to say that I have no magic wand to wave over your future and say, "All of a sudden everything is going to fall into place." Instead, you need a vision. Vision requires determination and believing in yourself, even in a world that is negative and hostile. Even in a world where the majority says, "We can't," you can.

What is your vision? What do you dream of achieving? What are some of your challenges? If you don't truly believe that you can do it, you're setting yourself up for failure. I'm sure it comes as no surprise to most of us that we act out precisely what we take in. In other words, we become what we think. You need to have a vision that is totally unique to your dreams. Don't let it be the dreams that others have for you. It has to come from you. It has to be your dream and vision. Don't ever lose sight of that dream. Focus on your vision and you will be able to achieve it.

I have to admit that during my hike up the mountain to achieve my goals, I often felt as if my dreams dissolved into a nightmare. My high hopes took a hike. Good intentions got lost in a comedy of errors, only this time nobody was laughing. I didn't soar; I slumped. Instead of pressing on to the top of the mountain, I felt as if I were in an avalanche thundering down the mountain. Let me tell you—discouragement is just plain awful. Discouragement may be awful, but it's not terminal. When we get discouraged, we temporarily lose our perspectives. We lose sight of our visions and dreams. Little bumps become mountains. A slight irritation, such as a pebble in a shoe, seems huge. Motivation is drained, and worst of all; hope departs. This is why you need to have a support system. I couldn't have achieved my goals without my faith in Jesus and the support of my family, friends, and husband. When I felt too overwhelmed or discouraged, they were there to get me back on track. They were there to cheer me on when I most needed it.

Hikers can't climb to the top of the mountain all by themselves. They need tools to help them climb to the top. They need ropes, spiked shoes, backpacks, tents, food, and they often climb with a partner. The same goes with our wanting to achieve our dreams. You need to find the appropriate tools to help you achieve your goals. You can't do it all by yourself. You need to find something or someone to be your "rope," your stronghold who will keep you from falling off the path too far. You need to find someone who will be your "tent," your safety net who will protect you from pessimistic elements. You need to find someone to be your "food," your daily source of encouragement. You need to find someone to be your "climbing partner," your constant companion and cheerleader who will be with you during the ups and during the downs. When you have all your "tools," you're ready to begin your hike.

Sometimes you need to take time and look back at all that you have accomplished already. Let's face it: graduating from high school is no easy task! You've already made it this far. Just think what you can all achieve! When you get discouraged, look back and list all your accomplishments. Then look forward again and continue working on your goals. Finally, always dream big! Even if at the moment you think they are unrealistic goals, go for it! The higher the goal, the more you'll achieve. If you limit yourself to safe little goals, where will that take you? Not as far as if you dream big dreams!

Okay, graduates, I ask you the same question that Nancy asked me: "Where do you see yourself in ten years?" Are you thinking big *enough? Create the vision, believe in yourself, want it, get the support you need, and most importantly, think* big*!*

As I looked out into the audience and saw my parents, my husband, and my counselor all smiling with pride, I finally realized that I don't need to do things on my own. I finally realized that to be truly strong, I need to be humble and ask for help. I'm the strongest when I'm the most vulnerable. I learned the true definition of strength, perseverance, love, and family. They are proud of me, and broken or whole, they love me for who I am. We have experienced the lowest, darkest valley of evilness, but God has certainly delivered us from evil … God has carried us to the top of the mountain, and the view up here is breathtaking!

Chapter 22

He has opened my eyes ...

Yes, I have always been a Christian and was raised to believe in God. I grew up learning the Bible stories and learning how God keeps His promises, how He never gives us more than we can handle, and that I'm forgiven. I even taught those lessons in Sunday school. My life was great and I never had reason to doubt what I was taught. For many years, those lessons never really sunk into my heart and mind. They just stayed on the surface.

However, when I was hiking this mountain of mine and going through the "valleys of darkness," God's faithfulness, love, and forgiveness were the only things that kept me going. Never before have I had my faith tested like this. Never before did I know what it's like to lose everything and have to rely on God for everything! Never before did my faith come so alive.

I wouldn't wish my experiences on anyone, but I wish all people could experience what it's like to have God's word come alive. At times when I was being raped, hurt, or humiliated, it seemed that God was very distant. However, it was during these times that He was the closest to me, holding me tight to Him and keeping me alive. He protected me from the pain of remembering all the horrible abuse I endured while I was a young child and gave me the gift of being able to dissociate and split. That gift kept me alive. He knew I was too young to deal with such trauma, but then he allowed me to remember when I was older and was strong enough to survive. At times, I wish He would have kept the secrets from me a little longer, and I doubted that I was strong enough to cope with all the pain, but His timing was perfect. God knew that I was strong enough, and He opened my eyes in time to keep my family and me safe from further pain.

I can't even imagine what would've happened to me or my family if God hadn't opened my eyes to all the memories. Yes, we endured much pain, but it could've been so much more. God's timing is impeccable. I sometimes wonder why He allowed so much to happen. Why not open my eyes after the first rape—or even before being raped? Why me? Why allow me to be hurt and terrified when I was just a little child? Why target my family? I do not have answers to these questions; I can only rely on faith that He had a reason.

Faith is such a tricky thing. "Faith is being sure of what we hope for and certain of what we do not see" (Hebrews 11:1 NIV). In order to have faith, you need to completely trust. Surviving what I survived, my trust in everything was shattered. I trusted that my parents would keep me safe. Unknown to them, I was not safe in the hands of Mr. Nelson. Being so young and naive, I believed the lies Mr. Nelson told me and was trained to think that my own parents would disown me. I lost all trust in my parents. I had trusted Mr. Nelson to be a loving and caring grandpa figure to me. He shattered all my trust quickly as he began to torment me.

I had trusted Sebastian and Stacy to be my friends, but they too soon shattered that trust as they betrayed me and left me in the evil hands of Coach Carl. I trusted Coach Carl, a teacher and a coach, to treat me respectfully. That trust was soon broken. I trusted the police to help me find justice and to put a stop to all this pain, but they too disappointed me. I trusted my athletic ability to be a way to escape the painful reality, but even that didn't help. I trusted that my thinking skills would help me outthink and outmaneuver my attackers, but I soon learned that even I couldn't predict their thinking or behavior. I trusted that since I was a "good Christian girl," I would be spared such evil. I felt as if everyone and everything I put my trust in quickly evaporated and left me all alone, helpless, terrified, and ashamed. I had trusted God that He would protect me in all circumstances, and at times, I felt as if He disowned me.

I'm often described as being stubborn and "difficult." Well, like everything else in my life, I tend to have to hit rock bottom before admitting that there's a problem. When all my sense of trust and faith were gone and I had truly hit rock bottom, that's when I finally realized what true faith is all about. I felt that God had forsaken me, yet He was the only one I could grasp on to. My experience opened my eyes to see just how much I needed Him. It is a difficult thing for me to put so much faith into something I cannot see, but I learned that even though I felt He had disowned me, He really didn't.

Being a teacher and even a mom, I see and experience how difficult it can be to stand back and watch a student or my own sons having to struggle a little while working through a difficult problem. I often want to rush in and alleviate that struggle for them and just do it for them. However, I don't rush in and fix it for them. I know that true learning comes from a little struggle and that they won't learn if I swoop in and do it for them. I imagine God being my teacher and watching me struggle with this test ... my test of faith. Like a good teacher, God knew that I would learn the most after struggling and persevering through a difficult test. And I like to think that since I'm so stubborn, He had to give me a pretty difficult test. It was probably difficult for Him to just sit back and watch me struggle and be in such pain, but with his omniscience, He knew the ending. He knew that I would persevere and come out so much stronger.

Since I was given such a difficult test, my faith got quite the workout. And just like an athlete in heavy-duty training, I grew stronger every day; I had faith in God that I would survive and overcome all this adversity. While running a marathon, the runners often have family members or supporters cheering them on from the sidelines. I also had my family members and supporters praying for me, encouraging me, and teaching me how to hold on to my faith.

My parents, relatives, and family friends surrounded me with God's promises and constantly reminded me of His faithfulness. The many prayer chains my family and I were on were a great reminder of the power of prayer. I was taught how to apply Scripture to my own life. The trials and temptations that many of the people in the Bible went through were similar to what I experienced. I could read how God used those trials to help those people, and I was able to see and have faith that God would do the same for me too. The scriptural truths weren't only skin deep now. They went all the way to my soul. After this experience, I can no longer look at God or the Bible or at my faith in the same way. He has opened my eyes … Hallelujah!

Abigail: Now, as an adult, I find myself sometimes wishing my faith could be as strong as it was when I was ten. So many people I talk to feel as if their faith didn't become real to them until they were adults and more mature. But for me, without a doubt, my faith became real and important to me at ten years old. I prayed for hours every night. I trusted God. I relied on God. I appreciated the small things. I rejoiced in the little victories in Rachel's recovery. I prayed with confidence. None of what happened to her ever made sense—why would God let this happen?—but I always knew things would work out. I didn't stress. Maybe it was my lack of maturity that helped me to have such a pure, childlike faith. But as I said, sometimes now as an adult, these are areas I struggle in.

Trust is a scary but wonderful thing …

After being so broken down and having my trust in everyone shattered, I vowed to never trust anyone ever again. I couldn't risk the chance of being disappointed once again. However, God sent some special people into my life who taught me that trust is not a four-letter word. I consider these special people to be angels sent from God because they were relentless in teaching me the beautiful gift of trust. They were the people I often hurt the most while I tested out my trust, and they persevered.

My first angel, Travis, taught me to face my fears and to trust the system. Travis was the peer counselor at my high school. He was a dear friend of mine and was a skilled listener who had a heart of gold. Without his friendship, I wouldn't have been brave enough to face the horrible truth of all that happened to me. He slowly gained my trust, and I began to tell him that I was being mistreated. Travis taught me to respect myself and understand that it wasn't right for me to be treated so poorly. With all the brainwashing from Mr. Nelson and from Coach Carl, it was difficult for me to acknowledge that I do deserve to be treated with respect. With Travis's incredible patience, persistence, and perseverance, he was able to convince me to open up and tell authorities that I had been raped. Without his friendship and his teaching me to trust him, I never would have told. I can't even think about what would have happened if I hadn't met Travis and trusted him. It was not a coincidence that I was friends with him. God put him in my life for a reason. God knew what I needed and provided it for me. This is just another example of how God was watching out for me!

My next angel, Naomi, taught me a lot about tough love and the power of prayer. Naomi was my faithful Christian counselor from the time I was fifteen until I was about twenty-two years old. During those years, we cried and laughed and learned to trust each other. I first met Naomi during one of my most unbecoming moments, yet she wasn't scared away. She was able to gain the trust of one of my younger personalities, which over the years was able to spread to all the others. I often played mind games and became hostile when working with Naomi, but she persevered and taught me how to trust through tough love. Among many things, she was a great teacher to me. She never ceased praying for me and with me, also teaching me how to combat all my fears with God's word. While working with Naomi, I could often see and even feel the power of prayer working. When I began working with her, I had a difficult time trusting my parents, so I thought of her as my surrogate mom. I no longer work with Naomi, but I still think, *What would Naomi think? What would Naomi pray about?* God truly worked miracles through Naomi. The work she did with me is nothing short of a miracle. Yes, it was extremely difficult work, and we both worked so hard that we cried, but God's love and power were evident throughout all those years. Thank God for counselors like Naomi!

Nancy, one of my teachers at Grantwood Alternative School, was an angel for putting up with me. She was my favorite teacher, yet I lashed out at her the most. Despite my violent episodes, she never gave up on me. She believed in me and taught me to believe in myself. Yes, my parents and relatives believed in me, but knowing that someone besides my family believed in my potential was a game changer. I tested Nancy, and she passed my test with flying colors. She didn't let me down, and I couldn't let her down. She inspired me to quit the facade that I was playing. It was time to get to business … time to regain control of my life … time to accomplish my dreams … time to be a conqueror! Thank you, Nancy, for being an angel and inspiring me to be a teacher like you—a teacher who doesn't give up on any child!

My most beloved angel, Derek, taught me the hardest lesson of trust: trusting someone enough to love. I met Derek my freshman year in college. This was the first time I was truly away from my parents and the first time experiencing true freedom. Desperately wanting to be normal and to have the college memories of other normal teens, I often pushed down memories and stuffed them in a faraway box. I was thinking that since it had been three years since I had been raped and since I had such intensive therapy, I thought I should be "over it" by now. I thought I was ready to put my past behind me and begin living.

When I first started college, I was on the college soccer team. All fall sports members and band members attended summer camp and began living on campus before school began. I would say that my first few months of my freshman year was my rebellious stage. During that first week of camp before school started, I met Neil, who was a goalie for the men's soccer team. Even though Neil was a "bad boy," we soon started dating. While with Neil, I often shook uncontrollably and was plagued with flashbacks. I was too scared and embarrassed to explain what was happening and would just avoid his questioning with, "I'm just cold." After several months of dating Neil and being scared to date and being with any male, I was set up on a blind date with Derek.

Our first date was on December 12, the day before the anniversary of my worst day ever. My parents were furious with me for going on a date with an older boy, a boy they had never met, a boy who lived a couple of hours away—especially since it was during my difficult time of year. Since I knew it upset them so much, I agreed to the date on

December 12 just to spite them. I knew they had little trust in me and my choice of guys to date, and I wanted to prove to them that I was okay and able to make my own choices. My rationale was that if it was a bad date, then I would still only have one bad time of the year. If it was a good date, then it could help take away the ugliness of December.

December 12, 1997, became one of the best days in my life. I met Derek, who is my angel here on Earth. On that first date, I could feel the walls around me beginning to chip away. I could feel myself feeling something for him, something I had never allowed myself to feel before: total trust in someone.

We began dating and seeing each other over Christmas break and on weekends. Derek made me feel comfortable and worthy. He treated me with respect, love, and patience. After several weeks, I began to tell him about my past and that I was raped. Besides feeling safe around Derek, I wanted to protect my heart. I wanted to let him know who I was—even the ugly side of me—before I really fell hard for him and ended up with a broken heart. Thankfully, Derek responded amazingly well and still wanted to date me. My brother Luke said that if Derek truly respected me, he would wait to kiss me until I was ready, even if it took four months. Well, it did take four months before I allowed Derek to kiss me, yet he still wanted to be with me.

I would like to say that the next three years were all rosy and that we never had any issues between us. However, that would be a big lie. Understandably, when I first met Derek, I had a lot of baggage to work through and the memories were still so raw. From our first date on, I felt safe being with Derek and knew I could trust him. Even though I felt safe and knew that I was safe, I still tested him. I would often try to upset Derek on purpose and even get physical with him so that I could see how he would react when he was angry. To my amazement, he never raised a hand to me, never said a disrespectful word to me, and never told me to get lost.

Derek taught me what true love is, the love that God described in 1 Corinthians 13:4–8 (NIV): "Love is patient, love is kind. It does not boast, it is not proud. It is not rude, it is not self-seeking, it is not easily angered, it keeps no record of wrongs. Love does not delight in evil, but rejoices with the truth. It always protects, always trusts, always hopes, always perseveres. Love never fails." Derek is so patient with me. He knows when something is wrong or bothering me, and even when I push him away and tell him that I'm fine or that nothing's wrong, he patiently waits for me to be ready to talk to him. He has never told me that it's time for me to be over my issues. He has never told me that what I'm thinking or feeling is silly.

For all the time I have known Derek, he has only treated me with kindness and respect. Even when I wrongly take out all my frustrations and past hurts on him, he is kind. He knows that my anger is not directed at him, and he often wraps his arms around me in a tight embrace. Derek does not hold any of my past or even present against me. When I ask him how he can love such a messed-up girl, Derek responds with a bewildered look, "I love you for who you are. I don't see a messed-up girl. I see an amazing woman … an amazing wife … an amazing mother … an amazing teacher … an amazing woman who has survived horrible things." Derek has heard everything I've gone through, has heard my parents talk about all the crazy things I did, yet that doesn't faze him. At times, I try to convince him that I'm too psycho to love and that I'm not worthy of his love; it's so painful for him to hear me talk about myself with such low self-worth.

Derek taught me that I can trust him enough to let down my guard and tall walls around me. Letting down those walls and trusting him so much is a very difficult thing to do. Just when I feel that I completely trust Derek, the smallest thing will make me put up those walls again. Since Derek works in the agriculture business, he doesn't have set work hours. His schedule changes every day, and it often changes from one minute to the next. When Derek is not home when he told me he'd be home, I often get scared and begin building walls around me. Flashbacks of being dropped off at the high school for a Saturday morning practice begin to wash over me, causing me to distrust him. Or when Derek is frustrated with the boys and begins to raise his voice, I immediately panic and back away from him. I know that my boys and I are safe, but memories of being yelled at by Mr. Nelson come racing back. Such little everyday occurrences are a reminder that I haven't completely learned to trust ... yet. *Yet* is such a tiny word but a powerful word. It means that I don't have 100 percent trust in Derek but that I'm still working on it and getting closer all the time. I'm not going to stop trusting him just because of a setback. I'm going to push on and continue learning how to trust wholeheartedly.

I have learned that I can trust Derek with my newly found emotions, with my hopes and dreams, and that I'm safe with him. Mr. Nelson created me to be his living dolly ... a doll void of all emotions. Learning to have, acknowledge, and experience emotions is a new and scary thing for me. Derek admits that he doesn't understand how someone could be without emotions, but he is very understanding when I experience emotions, often for the first time. I trust him that he is a safe person to experience my emotions with and that he won't be scared away or think differently about me. He helps me identify my emotions and doesn't take it personally when I sometimes displace my anger on him. He holds me and reassures me that it's okay to feel what I'm feeling and that I'm safe. I learned that when I trust him and open up to him, it is so freeing and a heavy weight is lifted off my shoulders. I realize that I don't need to carry this pain all by myself. Derek is my husband for better or for worse; he is my life partner, my rock, when I'm feeling weak. Derek has taught me the difficult lesson of unending love.

I am fearfully and wonderfully made ...

Derek has also taught me to have self-respect. Eventually, after hearing Derek tell me over and over that I'm a wonderful wife, a wonderful mother, and that I'm who God created, it slowly began to sink in. God wants me to be treated with respect. I don't deserve to be hurt. God wants me to love and respect myself. God doesn't want me to keep punishing myself for my past. He has already washed me clean by dying on the cross. His love and forgiveness are enough.

I thought I had to hurt myself and punish myself for all that I went through. I felt such shame and embarrassment. How could God still love me? How could I ever be forgiven? How could anyone ever love me? Why should I love me? I often hated myself. I was so disappointed in myself. I have slowly learned that such thoughts are not from God. Psalm 139:14 (NIV) says, "I praise you because I am fearfully and wonderfully made; your works are wonderful, I know that full well." When I have those ill thoughts about myself, I am slapping God in the face! God made me, and I am perfect in His eyes. God knew that forgiving myself and respecting who I am would be the hardest lesson I ever faced. He knew that I would need a husband who treated me with respect and who was relentless in teaching me to have self-respect. God blessed me with Derek, who is teaching me to view myself through the eyes of God. I *am* fearfully and wonderfully made!

"There's something about you ... something about the way the students respond to you ..."

Because of what I endured, I am the person I am today. I have a much deeper level of empathy for my children and students. When I have a student who has been labeled as a troubled kid or an anxious child, or a child who comes from a difficult home life, I embrace that child with an open mind. I put aside that child's past and focus on the child as a person, a child with promise, a child who is a survivor. I can relate to that child. That child doesn't want to be treated with pity. When I see that child, I see myself at that age. I can understand his anxiety, his behavior issues, his lack of trust, his low self-esteem, his displaced anger. I will always believe in that child. I will never give up on that child ... I want to be the Nancy in children's lives. I've been told by my administrators and students' parents, "There's something about you ... something about the way the students respond to you." I believe that it's because I have that special connection with the child who is hurting and the fact that I believe in that child and look past all the letters labeling that child.

My oldest son was diagnosed with autism at the age of three. I believe that my experience has given me a window into his mind. I believe that my experiences as a young child prepared me to be a parent of a child with autism. No, I am not autistic, but my experiences made me behave in a similar manner. I understand what it's like to be mute ...

not showing appropriate emotions … being lost in your own little world … being overly rough to get that sensory input. I understand my son, and I feel that we have a special connection. I have taught my son how to be successful despite his differences, and he has taught me to look at my childhood head-on and work on dealing with my past, no matter how painful it might be. We are a good team … We both push each other past comfort but are there for each other for much-needed support.

The father of lies

Sexual abuse is more than just an assault on the body; it's an assault against your body, emotions, mind, and spirit. When I was abused as a little girl, part of me was frozen in time. On the outside, I developed like a normal teenager, but on the inside, I was still that five-year-old dolly. As a teenager, and even as an adult, I believed the lies that Mr. Nelson and Coach Carl told me. The lies they told me were perceived to be true in those desperate situations. Being told repeatedly that I'm worthless, garbage, dirty, and too big of a sinner to ever be loved, the lies soaked into my mind and spirit and eventually flooded my mind into believing those lies. I didn't realize that they were using these lies to manipulate, brainwash, and intimidate me. I was blind to their programming me into being Dolly, or their living robot. Since I believed those lies as a young child, I continued to believe those lies when Coach Carl began hurting me. Without even realizing it, I had turned to my warped perception of truth. I believed I was too horrible of a sinner and too crazy to tell someone that I was being raped. They had programmed me into thinking and behaving exactly how they wanted me to respond. Young children are unable to comprehend the terrors of sexual abuse, and I thought that I did something wrong, that I was to be blamed.

Coach Carl, my homeroom teacher, and Detective Clark were able to see that I had childlike faith in authority and quickly took advantage of me. I highly doubt that if I were not abused in Georgia, I would have been raped as a teenager. On the outside, I wasn't the typical choice to be victimized. I had two loving parents, a loving family that did not have substance abuse issues, and I was a "good girl." However, during the interview process in middle school to be a part of the Discovery Program, I'm confident that my homeroom teacher quickly realized that something was amiss with me and selected me to be his new victim. I'm sure he caught on to the fact that I didn't remember my childhood and other red flags that indicated I was abused previously. He was an expert in manipulating me into believing all their lies.

Prisoner of their lies

I believed that it was my fault that I was abused. I believed that I deserved it and that if I were smarter or better, I could have prevented it from happening. To this day, I keep thinking and struggling with these thoughts: *What if I would have just told Mom about Mr. Nelson? What if I told Travis about the harassment right away? What if I didn't flirt with Sebastian? What if I didn't walk into the fine arts building that December night? What if I didn't wear that bodysuit that showed off my body? What if I were smarter and had been able to outsmart them? What if I fought more? What if I yelled and screamed more?* Being a young child and then a self-centered teenager, I believed that the world revolved around me. I thought that since something bad happened to me, it was a direct consequence of my behavior. I didn't realize that they had a premeditated, well-organized plan to entangle me in their web of abuse. As an adult, I still find it difficult to understand that it was not my fault; I couldn't have prevented it. I was just a teenager going against a group of master pedophiles. It's taken years of therapy for me to start accepting that I was the victim and had no control over what happened to me. No matter what I did, where I went, what I did or did not say, it was not my fault. It was out of my control.

I believed that it was my responsibility to keep my family happy. Mr. Nelson kept telling me that I was so naughty that my dad left and my mom was crying. I didn't want to see my mom cry, and I wanted my dad back home with us. I felt I had to be the perfect little girl so that my family could be back to normal. I believed that I had to be the "good little dolly" so that Mr. Nelson would be pleased and tell Mom that I was being good. I believed that I had to keep silent in order to help Mom and Dad feel better.

I believed that it was my responsibility to keep my family safe. I was threatened many times that if I told, my sister would be raped or that my little brother would be killed. My entire family and my friends were threatened on a daily basis, making me think that it was my responsibility to be silent and keep them safe. I thought that if I told, it would be my fault if they got hurt.

I believed that nobody would believe me—that I was crazy and too messed up to be taken seriously. I believed Detective Clark's and Coach Carl's lies that I needed to stay silent since no one would believe a "crazy teenager" like me. I thought that since they were adults, people would believe them and not me. I never even gave a thought to questioning them as to who was more believable: a well-known homicide detective or a teenager. When I first told my cousin over Christmas break that I was being harassed and my brother replied that I was probably just giving the guy the wrong idea, I believed their lies that I would never be believed. When I saw the pictures of my being raped, I believed their lies that people would think I was promiscuous. When the detectives told me to stop changing my story, I doubted myself. I believed that I was crazy and just making things up. However, once I finally got up the nerve to tell about being raped and Travis; the school nurse, Regina; and my parents believed me, I was able to see the lie for what it was—a big fat lie. People would believe me. I am telling the truth, and the truth shall set me free!

Since I was abused as a young child, my actions and attitudes are based on my past. At the age of four, I learned that when someone else was in control, I would get hurt. Mr. Nelson and his friend frequently reminded me and demonstrated that they were in control of my life. When I was in my coffin and being buried alive or trapped in the cage as I was being used as alligator bait, my life was in their hands. I was helpless, powerless, and forced into submission. Only they could pull me out … only they could change what was happening. When being raped at gunpoint as a fifteen-year-old, only Coach Carl and his friends were in control. When the doctor drugged me and my body went limp,

I was at their mercy. All my sense of control was taken from me. I was left having to beg for my life and rely on their help.

I ended up feeling weak, vulnerable, and exposed. To compensate for those feelings, I grabbed on to any sense of control that I could. I became manipulative to control things around me, hardworking to please people, obsessed with being perceived as being perfect, and a convincing actor to pretend that I was tough and that everything was okay.

I was made to feel powerless, so I yearned for some sort of control. I couldn't control what was done to me, so I began trying to control others. I became manipulative and played mind games with my family and therapists. I knew my parents' weak spots and would become very irate and irrational with them in order to get my way. Sometimes those times would come back and bite me, such as when I insisted on being dropped off for the Saturday morning basketball practice. The more I was told I couldn't do something, the more I would do just the opposite just to spite them, such as when I went on my first date with Derek. The more someone tries to persuade me to do something, the more likely I am to stick to my guns. I like to think that this strong stubbornness is a positive characteristic. I believe that this stubbornness helped me persevere and not give in to drugs, alcohol, promiscuity, and being a high school dropout. My abusers wanted me to be a failure and to remain under their control forever. I was determined not to let them win and to get the best of me. They won the first couple of rounds, but I got the final points. God gave me the fight in me to persevere and not lose hope. By God's grace, they have no power over me. I am a conqueror!

I believed that if I worked hard enough or was smart enough, I could've prevented and stopped the continuation of the abuse. I kept working harder and harder on my basketball skills, thinking that if I could just master those left-handed layups, I wouldn't get beat by Coach Carl. I practiced extra hard on my long shots and became the three-point master. The satisfaction of mastering the long shots was short-lived since no matter what I did, Coach Carl would still find something I did wrong. I kept thinking that if I was an A student, I could win the favor of my teachers and that they would help me be safe and believe me. Even though I *was* getting all As in my classes and was the role model student, the teachers still let me down and failed to protect me. I kept thinking that if I were the perfect Christian daughter, God would prevent all pain. I strived so hard to be that good girl and be worthy of going to church and God's forgiveness. After many years, I finally realized that no matter how hard I worked or how "good" I was, nothing would change the fact that I was hurt and needed help. As much as I prided myself on being independent and self-reliant, I now know that I need God's help. I need to give up control and trust God. He is the master of my life. He has a plan for me, and it's up to me to follow that plan. I finally learned that to be truly strong, I need to be vulnerable.

While trying so hard to be perfect, I learned how to put on a mask. In order to survive, I had to put on the mask that everything was fine. I couldn't let anyone know that I was being hurt. I couldn't let anyone know that I was terrified and depressed. I couldn't let anyone know that I was exhausted and wanted to curl up and die. Rather, I had to keep up my bubbly personality. I had to keep on living life strong. As complicated and embarrassing as it is to admit, I created various personalities to wear those different masks. I created a personality to be the fun and silly girl. I was dead inside, and it was impossible for me to continue being the fun Rachel, so this new personality took over for me. I created a personality to be the tough girl to protect me from all harm. This personality had a very high pain tolerance, which helped me endure the physical pain when I was too weak even to lift my head. I created a personality that was violent to scare everyone away or to hurt others before they hurt me. Although this personality was trying to help me, it often did the opposite. This personality did not trust *anyone* and would often break ribs or get violent with those trying to help me.

I created a personality to be flirtatious and sexual to protect myself from the guilt and shame that accompanied being raped while being videotaped. As hard as it was to understand how this personality helped me, I do realize that she prevented me from further emotional and physical pain.

I created a personality to be my comforter while I was lonely and scared at Mr. Nelson's house. I created a personality to be my mom when my real mom wasn't available. I created a personality to be Dolly to hold all those terrifying moments at the Nelsons' house. Whenever I needed to wear a different mask, I created a new personality. It's embarrassing, and I feel crazy to admit that I had different personalities, but it was truly a gift. They each took on the burden of holding the painful memories, and I was able to continue living as normally as possible. Yes, it's frustrating knowing that many of the attacks were able to occur since I had no memory of the previous attacks. But without this gift, I couldn't have survived. My brain wouldn't have been able to process all the trauma. Without the ability to split, I wouldn't have been able to have a normal childhood.

Through intensive therapy and many prayers, I became whole. I was able to integrate all my personalities and become wholly Rachel. It was a very sad day when I realized that I couldn't split anymore and that I had to hold onto all my memories myself. But I'm confident that the Lord has equipped me with the needed strength to face all my memories and fears. "Even though I walk through the valley of death, I will fear no evil, for you are with me, your rod and your staff they comfort me" Psalm 23:4 (NIV). As I continue working through the memories and emotions that each personality held on to, I'm beginning to remember more and more good memories of my childhood. It always catches me off guard when something triggers a happy childhood memory, making me hungry to regain all those forgotten years. "Rejoice in the Lord always. I will say it again: Rejoice! ... Whatever is true, whatever is noble, whatever is right, whatever is pure, whatever is lovely, whatever is admirable - if anything is excellent or praiseworthy - think about such things ... And the God of peace will be with you" Philippians 4:4–9 (NIV).

I wore many different masks and created personalities to wear those different masks just to appear "normal" and pretend that everything was okay. There are many people, abused or not abused, who create masks to hide their true pain. While at Esperanza Hospital in Dallas, Texas, I learned the importance of letting go of those masks and being real. There is no need for shame or embarrassment for feeling emotions.

Feeling emotions is a healthy step in recovery. As hard as I worked on mastering my masks, the more I secretly wanted someone to see past them and help me. I secretly wanted someone to see the pain I was in. I secretly wanted someone to look at me and say, "I know the mask you're wearing and I know you're in pain. It's okay to feel that pain. It's not your fault. Let me help you" … but very few people were willing to go down that road with me. While at the hospital in Dallas, I came across an anonymous poem titled "The Mask I Wear." Here is just a short sample of the poem, which can be found on the website www. community4me.com:

The Mask I Wear

Don't be fooled by me,
Don't be fooled by the face I wear
For I wear a mask. I wear a thousand masks-
Masks that I'm afraid to take off
And none of them are me.
Pretending is an art that's second nature with me
But don't be fooled,
For God's sake, don't be fooled.

Thank God for Travis, Naomi, Nancy, and Derek for seeing past my masks and being brave enough to walk down that scary path with me. As the poem says, please don't be fooled by the masks that people wear. When people say that they're fine or okay, most likely they are hurting and are too scared to ask for help. Instead of believing their facade, hold them tightly and be there for them.

The bondage of shame …

Even though it has been twenty-plus years since I was raped, the devastating effects of it still sometimes hold me in bondage. The hardest aspect to conquer is the shame. My family has a difficult time understanding the power of that shame. They don't understand why

I would have any shame; they keep saying that I have nothing to be ashamed about since it wasn't my fault. From their perspective, I agree with them. When I hear about others who have been raped or abused, I agree with my family that there is nothing for them to feel ashamed about. However, my shame is so entangled in the lies I believed about myself ... that it was my fault.

This shame is the hardest emotion to face and talk about since it eats away at the deepest part of my soul. It exposes the raw memories for what they are, which can be overwhelming, to say the least. That shame quickly turns into self-hatred. I hated looking at myself in the mirror since right there in front of my face is who I thought I was. When I looked in the mirror, I saw all their lies that I'm garbage, dirty, guilty, and too sinful to be forgiven. I used to become full of rage when looking in the mirror; I wanted to slash myself. I never broke a mirror as I so wanted to, but I did lash out at myself by doing self-harm.

I never wanted to do self-harm, but I felt compelled to do it. I felt I needed to punish myself. I never cut myself with the intention of killing myself. I did it to try to cope with my memories and emotions. At first, I cut myself as a distraction from the physical and emotional pain. I was able to focus all my attention on planning how to hurt myself, allowing myself to dissociate or zone out from the pain. I was so focused on the self-harm that I didn't look at the memories. It helped keep those painful memories locked in a box in the far corner of my mind. But then, I was always so numb and unable to feel anything; I was living like a robot. As much as I appreciated being able to zone out and escape reality, I was scared that I was so numb. I felt vulnerable, so I began cutting myself to feel something, even if it meant feeling physical pain. This is when it got scary and dangerous, for the more I hurt myself, the more I couldn't feel it. Since all sense of control was taken from me, I was desperate to have some control. I wanted to feel control over my emotions and pain. The ability to express and understand emotions was taken from me as a young child, so I was often confused and scared when feeling anger, sadness, guilt, and shame. I wanted to control the type of pain I would endure and when it would be done. I felt in control when I got to choose my cutting tool and when I got to choose the place and timing. My inward pain was building up and up and about to burst, so I released that pressure the only way I knew how: by doing self harm. Seeing the effects of self-harm gave me permission to cry. When I saw that I was physically bleeding, I finally felt it was okay to cry. I'm saddened by the fact that I needed that physical concrete image to finally give myself permission to feel sad.

For a long time, I did self-harm to feel better, but as soon as I did it, I felt even more ashamed, crazy, and confused, and I would continue the vicious addicting cycle. I finally realized that self-harm would never heal my deep, deep pain. The only way to heal completely from the inside out is to face those memories and emotions head-on. The more I push memories down, the more power I give my abusers and the more power the memories have over me. Each time I face a memory and talk about it, the less scary it is. After working through the memories, I am empowered and don't have any desire to do self-harm. "To you, O Lord, I lift up my soul; in you I trust, O my God. Do not let me be put to shame, nor let my enemies triumph over me. No one whose hope is in you will ever be put to shame" Psalm 25:1–3 (NIV).

Chapter 23

Frequently Asked Questions

How did your family overcome such obstacles?

I believe that we were able to survive because of God's grace, how our family bonded together, being on multiple prayer chains, and the power of prayer. I also believe that how my parents raised me helped me persevere. Perseverance is such a key component in survival. When I had a question or had a problem, they never swooped in and fixed it for me. Rather, they helped me form a plan to try, and if that didn't work, they would help me revamp the plan. My dad was always great at using the Socratic method. He would answer my questions by asking me questions that would help me solve the problem. As frustrating as it would be to not get a quick or straight answer, in the end, I'm so thankful.

As a teacher, I have seen how parents with good intentions have unknowingly taught their children how to give up. When they see that their children are struggling, they swoop in and fix the problems. In essence, they are teaching their children that they are not strong enough, smart enough, or capable of resolving their own problems. When such children are faced with difficult situations, they often panic and do not know how to handle the situation. They often give up easily and are afraid to take risks. I was raised to take responsibility for my actions (good or bad) and understand that it's good to try new things.

If the first attempt didn't work, try, try, try again. The word *fail* is just the *first attempt in learning*, not the end.

Abigail: Simple answer: God. My goodness, I have no other explanation. What Rachel lived through, experienced, and finally came forward and told, going through the last twenty years of recovery and moving forward … The only way Rachel survived any of it is by God's grace. How Mom and Dad as parents could endure the worst heartache imaginable and watch their child suffer extreme physical, sexual, and mental trauma … The only explanation is God. There were other factors too, orchestrated by God, that I feel played very important roles. Certain people placed in our lives, family, and the shared faith and love and support of our family were hugely important. God, faith, family, and laughter. Our family laughs a lot!

Did you ever prosecute your rapists?

No. We pressed charges against Shawn, and he was held in juvenile detention until we dropped the case. We were advised to drop the case since it got so complicated, I was not emotionally fit to endure a trial, and it put my entire family's safety in jeopardy. At times, I wish we would have taken them all to court to try to get justice and prevent them from hurting any more girls. However, there was no way I would have been able to testify and be badgered by the defense attorney. At that time, I was having too many flashbacks and would split into different personalities. I would not have made a good witness.

Do you still have multiple personalities? Or the ability to split?

No. With intense therapy and lots of hard work, I am completely integrated and just Rachel. It was very difficult for me to let go of the various personalities since they were a great survival tool and they held all the difficult memories for me. At times, I wish I could still split since they held all the pain and I could live my oblivious life. Some personalities had special talents that I'd really like to tap into now, such as being fluent in Spanish and knowing sign language. On the flip side, there were personalities that I was happy to get rid of (the violent and promiscuous ones!).

I'm still trying to grasp the idea of who Rachel is and how to live a "normal" life. The hardest question for me to answer is how to describe myself. I feel that when I explain who I am, I am contradicting myself all the time and that I don't know who I am. Is that Rachel or a part of a different personality? When integrating into just Rachel, I now have characteristics of many of my different personalities ... I am very serious and practical, yet I love to have fun, be silly, and be idealistic. I still have that tough girl attitude, but I will be the first one to cry when listening to other people's problems. My students often see me cry when I'm so proud of them or when they confide in me, yet I allow very few people to see me cry about my own experiences.

Do you have any regrets?

I want to live my life with no regrets. Are there things I wish I would've done differently? Do I wish that I would've told my parents as soon as things felt creepy? Absolutely. However, looking back at what was done is like looking back with twenty-twenty vision. Since it had already happened, when I look back, I can see all the things I missed. But when in that moment, when I was facing evil in the eye and facing death head-on, I did what I needed to do in order to survive. Have I learned from my mistakes and experiences? Yes. Do I regret my choices and decisions? No.

Have you forgiven your abusers? Is it necessary to forgive them?

It depends on your definition of forgiveness. Was it right for them to hurt me? No. Have I forgotten what was done to me? No. Am I bitter and angry at them for all the pain they did to me? No. I will not give them that power over me! I don't know if it's right or wrong or if I'm just avoiding those emotions, but I honestly feel nothing toward them. I've accepted what was done to me, and I feel at peace. Life is too short to hold on to anger and bitterness. God has granted me peace and a passion for life. It's not up to me to judge my abusers. God is the final judge.

Would you ever go back to Georgia or your high school?

Yes. When I was pregnant with my second son, my therapist and I went back to visit my hometown and high school. I was nervous, and my husband was apprehensive about my going. He was worried about my safety. Even though I was skeptical about this trip, I felt I needed to face my fears head-on. And I'm so glad that I went. While walking the hallways of my former high school and my other places of horror, I was filled with an unexplainable sense of peace that could only be from God. All my fears and trepidations washed away, and I was able to stand firmly on my two feet and face all my memories with an awesome sense of peace and power. That trip was a defining moment in my recovery ... What happened to me in those places was horrible and frightening, but that fear does not own me. God is my refuge and strength. Now when I think about those places, I can see the whole picture: the bad things that happened but also the good things. And the good things are more prominent than the bad.

Did your mom or dad have any idea about the abuse in Georgia?

At the time, my parents had no idea. Most of the abuse that happened in Georgia was mental and I never had bruises. Looking back, I had some red flags such as bed wetting until I was eleven, playing oddly with my dolls, biting, showing inappropriate emotions, and showing very little pain. It always concerned my mom that I was so stoic when experiencing what should have been a painful occurrence. The only thing that has really haunted my mom is a picture that was taken of me when I was in Georgia. When my brother had his school picture taken, Mom had professional pictures taken of me, too. That picture of me shows Dolly...a little girl who is so forlorn looking with a tear in her eye. My eyes are lifeless with unmistakable sadness. That picture shows such a drastic difference from the Rachel my parents knew, and Mom could never figure out why I was so sad in that photograph.

Tools that helped me on my hike

As I've mentioned before, hikers need tools to help them get to the top of the mountain. Besides the support of my family, friends, and God's grace, I learned some helpful tools to help me cope:

Pet therapy

Our German shepherd mix, Sophie, was very helpful to me. Her calm and affectionate demeanor helped me calm down. Being able to pet her soft fur helped to ground me in the present. She seemed to know exactly what I needed: the occasional lick to remind me that I'm in the present and safe, the gentle but excited nose bump to take her for a walk, and her being my constant companion keeping me safe. When I was going through some rough moments and was feeling angry, I would absentmindedly pull out her whiskers. She never growled or showed her teeth; she would just lie next to me with her head on my lap. When I was feeling overwhelmed with sadness, I could bury my face in her fur and cry. She was my faithful friend who loved me no matter what I said or did.

Even to this day, I value the benefits of pet therapy. It's just so comforting to be able to pet and cuddle with a dog … Facing memories is so much easier when you can be preoccupied petting a dog. Even today, as soon as I pet my dog, I can feel my heartbeat go back to normal, and I can feel my body relax. My sixty-five-pound black lab mix loves to cuddle and lie on my lap; the weight of her sprawled across me, feeling her body go up and down as she breathes, and being able to stroke her fur has such a calming effect on me. Having a dog also helps me deal with the days when I don't want to do anything or feel depressed. Just knowing that my dog needs to be taken care of makes me get out of bed. When she brings me my tennis shoes and is jumping around with excitement, it encourages me to get outside and take her for a walk. Often, just the change of scenery helps me get out of my slump. The hardest part is getting up and walking through the door; once I'm outside walking my dog, I enjoy the moment and feel recharged.

Playing the piano

When I was a child, I took piano lessons for two years. I'm not gifted with the musical talents that the rest of my siblings inherited, and I'm often lovingly teased about my poor sense of rhythm, but I still enjoy playing the piano. My family can always tell what kind of mood I'm in by the choice of songs I play. When I'm feeling angry or that life is out of control, I often play the song "Sabre Dance." Actually, I don't play the song; it's more like I pound out the notes. Anger is an emotion that I still struggle with, and I don't know how to express it, so I often let it out through music. When I'm feeling discouraged or sad, I often play Mariah Carey's song "Hero." The words and melody speak to me and encourage me. Playing the piano has been a great source of expressing my emotions.

Journaling

When I met my first counselor, Dr. McConnell, I was introduced to journaling. I often was too scared to say things aloud, so journaling was a safe alternative way to face my memories. I often couldn't piece together all the fragmented pieces of my memories in my mind, but once I got them down on paper, I was able to put the puzzle together. When having a nightmare or flashback, I would often get stuck in that memory and freeze. Having a pen in my hand would help me break through that stronghold, and I could transfer that memory from my mind onto paper. Once it was on paper, I didn't have to continue looking at it. I could choose to go back and read the memory or I could choose never to look at it again. Writing my memories down gave me the sense of power I so craved. When journaling, I would write down my true feelings and write down the things I thought I could never admit or say aloud. I don't journal on a daily basis as I used to, but whenever I feel overwhelmed with emotions, I go back to my journal and write. Going back and reading my journal entries is also encouraging. I'm able to read how desperate I was and see how God was able to help me through those moments. I'm able to see the many prayers God has answered in my life and all the blessings He has given me. I wouldn't want to wallow too much in the past, but quick glimpses back are helpful. Because the rearview mirror in a car is smaller than the windshield, keep looking forward most of the time.

Being physically active

The discharge reports from each hospital I went to included the suggestion that I remain physically active. My doctors and therapists all saw my need to be physically active. Whether it was taking a walk or kicking a soccer ball around with my therapist, a lot of the hard work was done during this time. Doing something active was a great source of emotional release. To this day, I tend to open up more when being active, and I love being able to walk and talk through difficult things with my family or friends. I like the distraction of being able to talk while walking next to someone. Walking and talking is less threatening to me since we don't have to look at each other, and I can talk while looking forward. I feel less intimidated since it's a more casual conversation and I don't feel I'm being interviewed. I also like that every time my foot hits the ground, it is a constant way to ground me in the present. I feel that when I walk, I'm able to think more clearly and the numbing fog evaporates.

When I first told about being raped, my parents enrolled me in a self-defense class. I enjoyed this class and being able to express my anger by hitting and kicking a dummy. I was able to picture myself fighting back against all my attackers, and it gave me a great sense of power and control. However, once the class progressed to trying out our newly learned techniques against the padded instructor, I got too scared. When I saw the instructor pretending to attack me, I would have flashbacks and was too scared to continue class. When I took this class, the abuse was still happening and the threats were too realistic. I'm confident that if I would've taken this class later, once I was out of real danger, I would've been able to feel empowered.

When I was married and had my two boys, my friend and I took a kickboxing class. My friend would often comment that I was taking the class a lot more seriously than she was, and she marveled at how hard I would kick and punch the punching bag. She said it looked as if I were out to kill someone, and she was correct. I would take out all my aggression on that punching bag. I wasn't able to fight back when I was younger, but during that class, I pictured myself punching and kicking Shawn, Coach Carl, and Detective Clark. It was empowering, and I would leave class feeling peaceful. I didn't have to hold onto that anger, guilt, or shame. I could let it all out in class.

Holding an ice cube and drinking cold water

When going through a difficult flashback, my counselor Naomi would sometimes have me hold an ice cube. The coldness would keep me in the present and I would know that I was safe; that memory was then, this is now. When I was dissociating or getting violent, she would place an ice cube in my hand, which would jolt me back to reality. I would squeeze that ice cube and watch the ice slowly melt and drip through my clenched fist. By the time the ice cube was completely melted, my body would relax, my fist would unclench, and I would be able to talk and behave appropriately. As time went on, a drink of cold water would work just as well. Holding on to ice is my first go-to tool for myself and for my students who are angry. I had a student who was very angry and violent so the police had to be called. After a long struggle, she was finally in the police car. While the police officer was filling out his report and talking to the other school staff members, I went over to the police car door and talked to my student. I could see that she wasn't in the present and I saw myself in her, so I went and got an ice cube for her to hold. Thankfully, she took the ice cube and didn't throw it at me. She held on to it and squeezed it as hard as she could; she began laughing as the water dripped down her shorts and onto her legs. She was able to calm down, talk about the deer I pointed out to her as it crossed the road, ask for a drink of water, and smile as she gave me a high five. I was thrilled and relieved to see that the ice cube worked so well with her. After that incident, whenever she felt angry or out of control, she would ask for an ice cube.

Tearing things up

When I was trying to figure out my different emotions, I would have so many confusing and strong emotions just boiling up inside of me, and I had no way to relieve that pressure. I felt as if I were hot lava that was building up and up and boiling and about to erupt. I needed to release that tension before the volcano erupted into violence against others or myself, so I turned to tearing things up. This may sound violent and destructive, but I was given things such as old telephone books, scrap paper, cardboard, fabric, and Koosh balls to tear up. My counselors and parents realized that if I didn't have this release of tension, I would end up hurting myself; tearing up paper was a much safer alternative! My favorite thing to tear up was old denim … I loved that it was harder to tear, and I loved the ripping sound it would make.

Tips for teachers or family members

- Don't take the behavior personally (I was the most violent with those I felt I could trust).
- Be patient and talk in a calm voice (a raised or angry voice can trigger flashbacks).
- Don't give up on a child. (Labels are just letters. The label doesn't define the whole child.)
- Offer to listen … Don't pressure someone to talk (let the child or family member know that he or she is in control).
- Avoid power struggles (give them choices; let them have control).
- Don't judge a child or family. You don't know how you would've responded to an event until you are in that situation. Everyone is trying his or her best to survive.
- Listen and be aware of what is going on.
- You don't have to have all the answers, but be as honest as possible. If you don't know an answer, it's okay to admit that.
- Don't ignore bully behavior. Don't believe that "boys will be boys."
- Be predictable. Have the same routines.
- Teach students to persevere and to have resilience.
- Offer students hope; show them that you care.
- Treat every day as a new day; don't hold grudges.
- Create boundaries—troubled teens are very manipulative!

Ever since my dad and I talked at Denny's and I heard his famous saying, "We're at the top of the mountain," I've related my healing to climbing a mountain. At first, this mountain of pain was enormous, ominous, and daunting. But with every step, the mountain seemed less daunting and I was beginning to see the beauty in life again. At times, it seemed I was buried in an avalanche of memories and that I was buried too deep to ever dig myself out, but God gave me the power to persevere. I had many setbacks along my hike to recovery, but I didn't give up. My family and I often joke that I would take three steps forward and then fall two steps back. I won't lie to you and say that it was an easy hike ... Far from it! Recovering from such abuse and being able to live a happy life will probably be the most difficult thing I will ever have to endure. There were many times when I would be so physically, emotionally, and spiritually drained that I literally could not pick up my head from my pillow. There have been times when I cried so hard I was scared I wouldn't stop. But being the gracious, loving, and all-knowing God, He knew when I needed a respite. He would often give me a glance at what peaceful life is like. When I was tired out or feeling forsaken, He would often give me something to smile about and give me a sign that I would be okay. He would lift the dense fog and let me see and feel His love and power over evil.

Yes, I worked very hard at recovering from all of the trauma, but I didn't do it alone. I had my family's constant support, empathetic friends who brightened my day, great counselors who pushed me to my limits, and many faithful people praying for me and my family. They all helped me deal with my memories, the anger, sadness, guilt, shame, denial, shock, and all the other emotions I learned to experience. They helped me have a sense of humor that only we could understand. We were able to find humor amongst the bleakest times. Having a sense of humor during these difficult times is so important. Laughing is a great way to release built-up emotions, and it helped me refocus and get a clear perspective on things. It helped me get "unstuck" in the most difficult memories, propelling me forward on my hike to recovery.

I have been on this hike of mine for more than twenty years, and I'm still plugging along. I have been to the summit and seen the beauty of life. The view from the summit is so breathtaking and worth every tear I cried during the hike to recovery. The peace, true happiness, freedom, and power I feel is unexplainable. Never in my wildest dreams did I ever think I'd feel this way! I feel so free and lighthearted. My past is not weighing me down anymore. I'm not under their bondage or their power. I'm free! Philippians 4:4–7 (NIV) says, "Rejoice in the Lord always. I will say it again: Rejoice! Let your gentleness be evident to all. The Lord is near. Do not be anxious about anything, but in everything, by prayer and petition, with thanksgiving, present your requests to God. And the peace of God, which transcends all understanding, will guard your hearts and your minds in Christ Jesus."

Is my life perfect? Am I always happy? No. Life will never be perfect until I am in heaven. But I am confident that I am strong enough to cope with anything that God throws my way. Do I still have my moments of self-doubt and feelings of shame or believe their lies? Absolutely. But I don't get stuck there. They are momentary bumps in the road. The road to healing from abuse is a long and tricky journey. Will the memories ever completely go away? No. They are a part of my life, and I embrace them for making me the person I am today. I am so much stronger, empathic, and devoted to my faith than I ever would be if I weren't abused. My life motto has been Jeremiah 29:11: "For I know the plans I have for you, declares the Lord, plans to prosper you and not to harm you, plans to give you hope and a future" (NIV). I probably wouldn't have chosen this journey to travel, but God had plans for me. He knew that I would persevere and come out stronger than ever. We may not ever fully understand why God led me down this path, and why it was as difficult as it was, but I thank God for the many blessings He has given me. I am filled with hope, peace, happiness, and excitement for the future that lies before me.

The hardest step of my recovery is forgiving myself. I often compare myself to others and think that I'm the worst person ever. I find myself comparing my parenting to others, comparing my faith to others, comparing my marriage to others … When people compare something, there is usually something that is better and something that is worse. As my counselor told me, "You're no better or no worse than anyone else." We all have our own unique experiences that shape our lives, perspectives, and behaviors. I need to stop comparing myself to others since no one has the exact same experiences. I need to realize that I'm already forgiven. Jesus has washed me clean with His blood on the cross. I *am* forgiven. I *am* lovable. I *am* worthy of good things. I *am* a child of God and perfect in *His* eyes. I *am* capable of facing my fears. "I can do everything through Christ who gives me strength" (Philippians 4:13).

Printed in the United States
By Bookmasters